I0044877

Technology Tips
For
Small Business

Steven G. Atkinson

Copyright © 2007
Steven G. Atkinson

ISBN: 978-0-6151-4028-5

Published in conjunction with tt4sb.com
Chestertown, Maryland

All rights reserved. This publication may
not be reproduced, stored or transmitted
in any form. This includes electronic,
photocopying, recording or otherwise
without prior permission.

Steven G. Atkinson can be reached at:
sgatkinson@tt4sb.com

Technology Tips
For
Small Business

Table of Contents

INTRODUCTION
How Important is Technology to your Business

TELECOMMUNICATIONS
What is Telecommunications?   13
When is a Toll Free call not free?   15
What is the future of Toll Free numbers?   17
There's a beeping tone on the other end!   19
But All I want to do is use the phone!   21
How much does that call cost?   23
Do I have a Multi-line Telephone system?   25
Do they know where I am when I call?   27
Who manages the contracts?   29
Slam, Cram and Scam   31
What is TEM?   37
How reliable is your system?   39
Does your number mean anything?   41
Music on Hold – Is yours legal?   43
Adding or Removing service   47

CELL PHONES

What do you need your cell phone to do?   51
All Cell Phones are not created equal   55
What cell phone service plan is best?   57
Can I use my cell phone in the car?   59
Whose number is it?   61
Hello, I can't talk right now I'm at a funeral.   63
Can Cell Phones cause fires at gas pumps?   65
Cell Phone users shouldn't talk during a storm.   69
Is there a Cell Phone Directory?   71

VOIP

A New Telephone System?   77
How does VoIP work?   81
VoIP and Regulations   83
Is VoIP the right fit for Small Businesses?   85
Benefits and Drawbacks of VoIP?   87
VoIP and IP security   89
Misconceptions about VoIP   91
Questions when considering VoIP   93

SECURITY

Inventory Control – Do you know what your have?   99
Is your network diagramed?   101
Would you be ready for a software audit?   105
How important are your contacts?   107
10 Things to help secure your data   109
Are you your laptop's weakest link?   111
Does someone know more about you than you do?   113
Prevent yourself from Indentity Theft   115
Gone Phishing. How to not get caught!   117
Caution that bill may be only an advertisement!   121
Wireless Communications Privacy   123
Technology things to do, but sometimes don't!   127
Secure data on removable devices!   129
Has common sense been replaced by rushing?   131

OTHER STUFF

It's all in the Planning   135
Spring Ahead to Fall Back – DST   141
5 things to do after getting a new computer.   145
10 Hi-Tech items to consider.   147
What is RFID?   151
Saving Energy and using Technology   153
Using batteries safely   155
Working with and learning to use a 'gadget'   159
IM for Business?   161
Using IM in Business   163
Create an IM Policy   165
How's your consumer service?   167
You have reached …   169
How's your email etiquette?   171
May I help you? Thank You!   175

Introduction

How Important is Technology to your Business?

Technology is important to business. It seems that wherever you look there is some type of technology involved. Calls for service are received and made with telephones. Computers are used to create and manage projects, correspond with others and allow quick and easy bookkeeping. Cell phones allow us to conduct our business when we aren't in the office. Office Automation devices such as Fax machines, copiers and electronic time clocks assist us to achieve our goals. At night we may be setting a security alarm to protect the property and there should also be a fire alarm system as well.

The one thing to remember about technology it's just a tool to assist in getting our work done. Having technology in the office or on our person is no different than a carpenter with his hammer and tape measure. It's just a tool to do the job.

It doesn't matter that we may have the newest, greatest piece of software or a new cell phone or the fastest computer in the area. Having the wrong technology to do the job is just as bad as a carpenter trying to drive a nail with a screwdriver. It may be able to be done, but it takes a lot longer and is not done right. It's even worst if the correct tool is available, but not knowing how to use it, or not using it correctly.

Here are a couple things to consider when evaluating or purchasing any new technology.

Understand the business need and the product enough to be able to make an informed decision. Having a slick salesperson tell you that the product will improve your business shouldn't be enough information to make that decision. Their job is to sell. Sometimes it may pay to have an impartial expert evaluate the needs and benefits.

Once you've made the decision to purchase, make sure that the user, whether it's you or someone on the staff, has the proper training to use the product to its best benefits.

You don't have to have each member of your staffed trained by the expert trainer. You can always do a 'train the trainer'. That is train the person on your staff who will be using it the most then have that person train the others.

Training never ends. It's just like a carpenter with his saw he has to keep it sharp to keep it in use. As technology changes, you need to be trained on new or added features.

If you always remember that technology is a tool and that you need to know how to use it for it to be productive, the money that you spend will never appear to be waste.

At the same time technology can only do so much. It can't be used to correct the ills of the office. Managers still need to manage their staff and while it can assist in that task, it will never be able to replace good old human common sense.

Managers need to use technology not ask technology to do their job.

At the beginning of 2006 I began a Weblog or as it's more commonly known, a blog, called Technology Tips for Small Business. Those informational tidbits have been put together in a logical order for this book. Many have been edited and revisited since the original posting.

The primary purpose is to educate owners and office managers of small business about technology so they won't be scared of it. But it's also to know there's no reason not to go out and ask for expert assistance. To have more information is to be able to effectively use the tool.

This book is broken into five sections. The first has tips relating to what is commonly referred to as telecommunications or telecom. My feeling that terminology is incorrect and in actuality it is telephony. Whatever it's call the section deals with the office telephone.

The second section deals with cell phones. VoIP is the new trend in business communications; the third section deals with it.

The next section is titled security, but it deals with the aspects of what can be done to prevent information from falling into the hands of those not authorized to use it.

The final section is termed 'Other Stuff' and has tips that deal with other technology related stuff.

Telecommunications

What is Telecommunications?

Telecommunications as a word has its origins in Greek. It's a combination of 'tele' which means 'Far Off' and 'communications' which is an 'exchange of information'. In simplest terms telecommunications means a far off exchange of information.

Early forms of telecommunication include smoke signals and drums. Drums were used by natives in Africa, New Guinea and tropical America. Smoke signals were used by natives in America and China. One may think these were used to announce the presence of a camp. But often they were also passing along information about the camp.

Other early forms of telecommunications are signal flags and lights. More modern uses include the telegraph, telephone and data transmissions. Many have the same root word 'tele'.

Telecommunications doesn't have to be two-way. Radio and TV are forms of telecommunications and these only deliver information.

Telecommunications can be point-to-point, from one transmitter to one receiver or point-to-multipoint which is also known as broadcasting.

The basic elements of a telecommunications system are:

  a.)   a transmitter. This device will take the infor-
        mation to be communicated and produce a
        signal to be transported.

  b.)   a transmission medium, this could be over a
        wire or over the air using the airwaves. The
        transmission medium, by its physical nature,
        is likely to modify or degrade the signal on
        its path from the transmitter to the receiver.

  c.)   a receiver, which reverses any actions per-
        formed by the transmitter in the exact reverse
        order of the transmitter. The receiver can be
        designed to tolerate a significant degree of
        signal degradation.

Some developments in telecommunications:

Signal lights - Ancient times
Telegraph - 1835
Bell's Telephone - 1876
Telephone Switchboard - 1878
Telephone Switching – 1891
Rotary Dial - 1896
Touchtone - 1963
Nortel SL1 (Modern PBX) - 1970's
VoIP – 1995

When is a Toll Free call not free?

The answer is always. It really should be called Automatic Collect, since the one being called is the one accepting the charges.

There are also times when it's not free to the one placing the call. If calling a toll free number from a cell phone, the long distance charges are free, but you are still using cellular minutes.

If your business has a toll free number never call your business toll free number from a cell phone, use the local number. Otherwise you are paying for the call twice. The toll free cost and cellular minutes.

Encourage customers in your local area to use your local number instead of the toll free number. One way to do this is not putting the toll free number on local advertising. Depending on the toll free calling plan you may be charged long distance rates for that call.

It's surprising when you talk with some people they really believe that no one is paying for the telephone call. Are they thinking that the telephone carriers from the goodness of their hearts are allowing those calls to me made free?

I remember hearing a story that each day at noon the new receptionist would take her lunch at a corner desk. She would spend the lunch hour talking with her mother, who was watching an afternoon program. They would be discussing the show.

When the long-distance bill arrived, it showed a call from half way across the country, lasing just short of an hour everyday during the lunch period.

It didn't take the manager long to put the pieces together to discover that the new receptionist was the one receiving the calls. When the receptionist was asked about the call, she admitted to it. But she didn't see anything wrong.

Her answer, "My mother called me on the toll free number." It didn't register to her or her mother that the company was the one paying for the call. They both thought it was a <u>Free</u> call.

Whenever calling a number that looks like it's toll free, it's important to remember that all numbers that look like toll free numbers aren't. Some will begin charging after the first couple of minutes, just like a 900 number.

What is the future of Toll Free numbers?

Many users, especially those using residential services now have long-distance included in their standard package. Cell phone plans include calls that would be classified in the past as long-distance. Do businesses really need those special toll free numbers for their consumers to call? It's getting less likely.

Many marketing professionals recommend that one way to help increase business is to get a toll free number. But in this day where everything is based on ROI (Return On Investment), does it actually pay to have that toll free number. It might, but I think that you need to evaluate the cost over the return and not just take a marketing opinion. Maybe it's time for business to stop using it as a marketing tool.

One of the things that I have not been able to understand is why a non-profit requesting donations use toll free numbers. If they have some one willing to donate, wouldn't it be reasonable to think that the donor would be willing to pay the few extra cents to place the call in the first place.

It seems as if this is the classic robbing Peter to pay Paul. They will put a note on a prepaid envelope asking for you to place a stamp on it to defray cost, but hardly ever do they list a toll number to call to defray the telephone costs.

Will toll free numbers be around forever?

Will toll free numbers only be used for special circumstances?

These are questions that we will know the answers to as time passes. The one thing for certain, they will continue to be used for some time, just how long, is another question.

The way that things are heading it's possible that one day all calls will be made for a fix price throughout the United States and there won't be a need for a toll-free system.

There's a beeping tone on the other end!

Have you ever answered the telephone only to hear a series of beeps instead of a person's voice? It may not be as noticeable as it was a few years ago, or then again maybe it's even more common. Either way, more than likely, a Fax machine originated those tones.

What do you do when you hear them? One thing could be just to ignore them. Most Fax machines have a setting to retry sending the message, but it's usually only for three to five times. After the retries, the call will stop

But there is another thing you could do, depending on what features your telephone system are capable of performing. If you have call transfer, transfer the call to your fax machine.

Once it's answered, the two machines will communicate and both sides will be happy. Just be sure to contact the originating party to let them know you received their Fax in error.

There's also the case of what I call the disappearing Busy Signal. Years ago everyone knew the sound of a busy signal, Recently, I made an error in the forwarding of my cell phone. I ended up forwarding it to one that was already being forwarded to my mine.

I was talking with someone, who said that there must be a problem with my cell phone. I replied that there wasn't thinking they were talking about reaching an associate. At the time I didn't want to be bothered with incoming calls.

The person I was talking to me said the problem wasn't that it was reaching someone else, but every time my number was called they received a strange buuup, buuup type tone. The person had either never heard, or had forgotten the sound of a busy tone.

Voice mail, answering machines and call waiting have nearly caused the death of the busy tone. There has been an advantage to these devices. Since many times answering machines and voice mail systems will pick up after the fourth ring, telemarketers have set their systems to discontinue the call usually after three rings. Setting your system for six rings will allow you to know when someone may be calling you and not a sales call.

But all I want to do is use the phone!

Does it really matter what features you have on your telephone if you don't know how to use them? Sometimes additional features are more of a hindrance than a benefit. What do you need your telephone to do? Many times all you need to do is be able to answer or make calls. If that is the case all you need is a Plain Old Telephone Set.

One day, I responded to a service call. When I arrived, I asked the user to describe the problem. The answer, "I don't have a problem. This phone does. It has too many buttons. I don't know what they do, nor do I want to know. All I want to do is use the phone."

If the person had been the administrative assistant or office manager, I may have seen reasons to explain why they may need or want the extra features. Since it was the President of the company, if all he wanted to do was use the telephone, who was I to argue.

It turned out that there was a simple reason why he had the phone he did. The one placing the order for service, instead of asking what he wanted, simply decided that he needed the biggest, best telephone that was available. The salesman may have even suggested it.

Since he's the executive, let's give him the most expensive executive phone. There wasn't a thought given to ask him, it was just assumed.

Don't be afraid to ask the users what they want. Yes, you need to be prepared to explain the features. Explain what they can do to help do the job, and possibly what they could do to make it harder.

Sometimes to people trying to get a current job done seems more important than listening. But no one wants to spend more money or get less technology than what's needed.

How much does that call cost?

Probably more than you realize. The per minute charges from telephone carriers may be low, but you can't just say it only cost a few cents for your employee to have a personal telephone call. While the employee is on the telephone they are still on the payroll.

For a thirty (30) minute call you may be paying a carrier less than a dollar, but with a ten dollar an hour employee, it'll cost another five dollars and that's without factoring the cost of benefits.

I was once asked how much does it cost in lost production for a 5 minute personal call per day. I sat down to calculate the total and it even surprised me.

A couple of items needed to be agreed upon. First was the amount of pay. To make things simple the figure of 20 dollars an hour was the agreed upon amount. The next was the number of workdays in a year. We started with 52 weeks of 5 days, which equal 260. Vacation and Holidays came to 27 with a final of 230 workdays after a couple of days subtracted for sick time.

The cost for the 5 minute call per day for the year came to $383.33.

Of course there's no guarantee that an employee will be productive during those five minutes. It may be just as well to allow the employee those 5 minutes a day so that their mind may not be on something else, especially if that call is from their child who just arrived home from school.

Some managers though may not have any problem with employees talking for 10 or 15 minutes on personal calls. That's a manager's choice.

One of the things that may be forgotten is the internal call that friends at the same company make to each other. Those calls don't reach the public telephone network and may not show on any telephone reporting records, and could last an hour or more.

The telephone is not the only office technology that can cause lost production. The Internet is another. An employee may be checking personal email, using Instant Messaging or looking for information for a personal purchase, while on company time.

It's even thought that the Monday after Thanksgiving is the heaviest on-line shopping day of the year.

Why is that? It's the first day back to work after the holiday for many who do not have high-speed Internet at home.

The policy on personal use of technology is up to you and your Human Resource officer to decide. This would be part of a technology use policy.

Do I have a Multi-line telephone system?

Almost all businesses with more than a couple of telephones will have some type of Multi-line telephone system. How can you tell if you have one? Does the phone on your desk have a telephone number that also rings elsewhere? When you dial someone else in the company do you just dial an extension? When you dial someone not associated with your company do you have to dial an access number, usually a '9'? If the answer to any of these questions is YES then you have a Multi-line system.

How is a Multi-line system defined? The definition I'm using is a private telephone system sharing a common interface to the Public Switched Telephone Network (PSTN), including network and premises-based systems.

There are three major types of commercial telephone systems on the market today: Key systems, KSU-less phones and PBX systems. A fourth system developed from Internet technology is Voice over Internet Protocol or VoIP. VoIP is a growing technology, but it still has a way to grow before realizing the same levels as the ones listed, although the same issues exist.

A Key system uses a central control device called the key system unit (KSU) to provide features that are not available with ordinary phones. A central unit typically allows users to make calls to another in-office extension, and prevents others from accidentally picking up a line that is in use. Modern key systems also come standard with most features a business would expect, but they can also be less customizable than other systems.

A KSU-less system is one designed to provide many of the features of a small business phone system in a decentralized manner. The phones themselves contain the technology necessary to allow them to communicate with each other without requiring a central cabinet. These often offer fewer features than a KSU system.

A PBX (Private Branch eXchange) is a telephone switching system that interconnects telephone extensions to each other as well as to the PSTN. A PBX enables a telephone set to gain access to one of a group of shared trunks by dialing a prefix generally either an '8' or '9'. PBXs also include functions such as least cost routing, call forwarding, conference calling and call accounting. Modern PBXs use all-digital methods for switching, but may support both analog and digital telephones and lines as well as VoIP.

You could also have a system called a hosted PBX system. This type of system is available over the PSTN and delivers PBX functionality as a service, using equipment located in the premises of the telephone company's exchange. A business doesn't need PBX equipment and the telephone company can use the same switching equipment to service multiple hosting accounts.

Do they know where I am when I call?

There are certain requirements that need to be followed if you are making a call classified as 'telephone solicitation'. This is any telephone call that acts as an advertisement.

FCC rules says that telephone solicitation calls can only be made between the hours of 8 am and 9 pm of the called party. Calls or messages placed because of a consumer's prior business relation are not considered as solicitation calls. The established business relation is put to an end if the person called asks not to get any additional calls or after 18 months after the last transaction or 3 months after the last inquiry.

Those placing telephone solicitation calls are required to deliver their telephone number and name, or the telephone number and name of the company for which they are selling products. The telephone number displayed on a called party Caller-ID system must be one that when called during normal business hours the called party can ask to be removed from the list. It is against federal law to transmit a number and name that is different than the company for which the call is placed.

Who else needs to know who and where you are when you call. Do the emergency workers that are answering 911 calls know where you are? It's estimated that nearly ½ of the population either work, study or live behind Multi-Line telephone systems. These systems could be PBX's, Electronic Key Systems or even carrier services known as Centrex.

Many times it may not seem important that the 911 centers receives a correct callback number and location. They will ask for the information. But there has been times that lives were saved because this information was available. By not having it, life saving services were prevented from arriving in a timely matter.

When a call is received by a 911 center and the caller is unable to communicate, such as having a heart attack and not able to breath or talk, the procedure is to have an emergency responder report to the location that is given to them.

At a small location, where all of the workers are near one another, a search for an incapacitated person may be easy. If there are multiple locations the emergency response team may be dispatched miles away from the actual emergency.

Another problem that could occur is the actual number a person uses to dial 911. Many Multi-Line systems require an access code to be able to dial an off-site number. When dialing 911, is that code needed? Is the telephone labeled as such, so that a person not familiar with the system can dial 911.

With Multi-Line systems, it's possible to prohibit a telephone from dialing outside numbers. It could be an accident waiting to happen if a telephone is restricted from dialing 911. These things are sometimes overlooked when putting in a system.

Who manages the contracts?

Whether you are in the process of purchasing a technology product or a service, you will need a vendor. But who controls that relationship. A vendor will want it to be them, but you are the one that needs to manage the relationship.

Many small businesses owners and managers will have maintenance contracts in place. It's not wise to let them wait idle until you need them, by doing so may delay a needed action.

The following will help in assuring that you will not lose control. While these tips relate to long-term contracts, usually maintenance or service providers, these are also important in the procurement process.

1) Ensure you have the contact information of the people within the vendor's organization whom you may need to contact. These people should represent work groups such as account management, sales support, billing, repair, and provisioning.

2) Set-up periodic meetings to discuss any issues that either group may need to resolve. How often and how long will depend upon each organization's requirements. The meeting could be as simple as a

telephone conversation with the account represent-
ative to ensure contact information is still correct.

3) Implement performance review meetings. How often
    these meetings occur would depend on the length of
    the contact. For example with a three-year contact, a
    performance meeting may not be needed more than
    once a year, but for a system purchase, it may be
    needed weekly. Treat these meetings just as you
    would treat an employee review with quantifiable
    objectives listed and measured.

While we are talking about service contacts it's not unusual
for telecommunications invoices to have errors. It is for that
reason that they should be checked each month before payment is made.

Many vendors require written notification of disputed
charges and authorization allowing short payment of
amounts due. Without the proper contacts in place, it's hard
to know where to go with the concerns.

Proper documentation can and usually will protect you.
Short payment of invoices may look upon as non-payment
and late charges can be assessed on those amounts. Should
at some time a disconnection be threatened, the correct
documents give a paper trail that can be used to substantiate
your actions.

Slam, Cram and Scam

Does it ever seem as if there's always someone trying to get your money? Even in telecommunications it's that way. Some people may be trying to get your money to help your business, such as consultants, while others are nothing more than crooks trying to steal.

Here are some helpful tips to try to keep your money in your pocket. Some of these may seem like ancient history, but could still happen.

Don't be slammed.
Slamming is when your long-distance telephone service is switched to another company without your permission. This could happen in many ways, it could be in the form of what appears to be a check and cashing it will allow them to change your present service to theirs, usually at a much higher rate. Another way is to receive a telephone call offering you lower rates, even declining the service you may have been switched.

Watch for Cramming.
Cramming is when optional services such as voice mail, paging, a personal 800 numbers or club membership appears on your telephone bill. This can happen, like slamming, by filling out a contest entry form, failing to respond to a nega-tive option sales pitch, or calling a 900 number. It can hap-

pen simply by the crammer picking your telephone number out of the blue and placing charges on your bill through your local telephone company claiming that you agreed to purchase the services.

Be aware of scams.
Two of the most commonly known ones are the "809 area code" and the "90#" scams. There are others such as the Collect Call scam and the *72 scam.

The "809" scam is real, but four important pieces of information to keep in mind are:

- Not every phone number in the 809 area code is part of this scam, and calling such a number will not necessarily result in exorbitantly large charges on your phone bill. Those numbers that are part of the scam are actually charging you a pay-per-call service, similar to a 900 number. Most 809 numbers are ordinary, legitimate phone numbers.

- This scam has been used with other area codes besides 809. Other area codes associated with this are 284 and 876. 809 is a Dominican Republic code, 284 is the British Virgin Islands and 876 is Jamaica.

- The amounts of money involved have been greatly exaggerated as this warning has circulated on the Internet over the past several years.

- This scam is not very common; the average U.S. user is unlikely to ever encounter it.

The "809" scam works because they are outside of US they are not under any US regulations. To avoid falling prey to this scam or any that may come from calling a pay-per-call service is to know where you are calling before dialing the number. When receiving a message from someone you don't know the best thing is to simply disregard it.

The "90#" is also true, but only to a degree. It only works on systems that require a user to dial a '9' for an outside line and there aren't any other restrictions placed on the service.

For those businesses that require dialing a '9' for an outside call by dialing "nine-zero-pound" the caller may be transferred to an outside operator where a call could be placed to anywhere in the world. The call would then be charged to the business' phone bill.

Any other method of dialing out, whether it's because it's a direct outside number where you simply dial the telephone number, or use another digit, such as an '8' for an outside line, this scam would not work.

Some telephone systems restrict the system from dialing a long distance call once you have accessed an outside line, local numbers may be the only option, this will not work either.

Both of these are so old and have been passed around in emails as being new a few times a year, that it is doubtful that anyone would really try to use either of these scams. But there are always dumb crooks, so it's good to be aware.

The Collect Call scam works when you accept a call from an operator asking to accept an urgent collect call. Once the call is accepted, you are billed for the collect call charges.

The best policy is to never accept collect calls. If you do only do so if you have exact knowledge on who the person is placing the collect call. Collect calls can have a high cost and most times, there are more reasonable calling methods.

Another newer and perhaps more dangerous scam is called the *72 scam. This scam seems to come from prisons and may be associated with collect calls.

A collect call is received and the caller convinces the recipient to entering the code *72 followed by a number after they hang up. *72 is a common code for call forward, and now your number is forwarded to the number you entered. This allows the person placing the call to make a second collect call, only this time reaching the forwarded party, who accepts the charges. The charges will appear on your bill.

Toll fraud.
This occurs when someone charges their long-distance calls to your number. This could be because your calling card is stolen, or your account number is obtained by someone looking over your shoulder at a pay phone. An unsecured telephone system could also be hacked into for someone to use your telephone service for their calls. Voice mail systems have been known to have security flaws.

Watch the cost of Prepaid phone cards.
Prepaid phone cards are sometimes worthless or more expensive to use than coins, if you can find a payphone, or collect calls.

Beware of cards that do not come with clear information about the rates for the calls. Comparison shop for the best rates and find out if there are fees or surcharges that might apply.

Some cards may have a minimum that is used by each call or fees such as connection and maintenance. Most will also charge extra if the call is made from a payphone.

Other things to look for is how the per minute charges are rounded, such as rounding to the next minute. Some round to as much as five minutes even if only one additional second is used.

Know when the card expires. Also check for Taxes and Surcharge. A low per minute rate could mean a high surcharge.

Not all 800 numbers are toll-free.
You can be charged for calling an 800 number if you have agreed in advance. But some consumers are tricked into being charged for 800 numbers by following instructions to dial "personal activation codes" that are really access codes linking them to "pay-per-call" numbers.

Be aware of the price of the call.
Services such as "pay-per-call" and 900 calls may not be worth the price of the call. When you dial a "pay-per-call"

number that will cost more than $2, you must be told the company's name, the cost of the call, what will be provided, that kids under the age of 18 need their parents' permission to stay on the line, and that you can hang up when you hear a signal without being charged. You can put a block on your telephone system to prevent people from making 900 number calls.

Beware of fraudulent computer-generated charges.
One twist to telephone frauds is related to programs downloaded from the Internet to view pictures. Later huge telephone bills are received for international calls. They did not know that the viewer program was designed to disconnect their computers from their regular dial-up Internet service providers and reconnect them to the Internet through an International telephone number.

The lesson here is don't download programs from web sites unless you know and trust them. This is also one of the places where entering your telephone number into a form may authorize a company to place a recurring charge on your telephone bill for a service such as club memberships or voice mail. It's important to read the terms of agreement.

Because of these types of charges it's important that the telephone bill is checked each and every month. You have the right to dispute any charges you do not agree, but you should put those reasons in writing.

What is TEM?

A new buzzword in the telecommunications community is TEM. What is it? It's not TEAM without an 'A'. TEM is one of those acronyms that depends on the field you are in as to what it means.

If you work in biology it would stand for Transmission Electron Microscopy. In environmental studies it's a Terrestrial Ecosystem Model. In telecommunications, it stands for Telecom Expense Management.

There may be just as many TEM vendors as there are services they provide. Some claim they will increase savings by doing a one time evaluation and recommendation. Others will say they can reduce the hassles of managing your telephony expenses. Still others will want to manage your telecommunications enterprise.

But TEM really should be thought as Technology Expense Management. It may be a wise decision to consider the need to manage the entire technology infrastructure.

There are many technology related items that you use that have a cost. Some of them like your telephone system, Internet connection, and cell phone and copiers usually have a monthly cost.

Even if it doesn't have a monthly cost, there still is a cost. There's a purchase cost, an upgrade cost or replacement cost.

Technology Consultants are the ones to fill those needs. I've seen it recommended that one of the top technology items needed for your business is a local technology consultant.

All TEM vendors are really nothing more than Technology Consultants. They just may focus on a specific technology item.

When using a TEM vendor it is important that everyone understand your business model. Some of the areas that a TEM vendor may address are;
- Control of Expenses
- Asset Management
- Determine Telecom Cost
- Invoice Processing
- Reporting of Trends

Is it time to step back and evaluate your technology cost? Those costs may be a much greater chunk of your expenses than you may realize.

Many businesses wouldn't work without an accountant or a lawyer on retainer. Maybe it's also time to have a Technology Consultant on your team as well.

How reliable is your system?

The average business owner doesn't always understand what is meant by terms that are thrown at them.

Have you heard about five nines? If you haven't, you haven't been listening to your telecommunication vendor. It's a real catch phrase with them.

But what is Five Nines?

What does it really mean?

For those who have heard it, you know that it refers to the reliability of the system. It's most often used to discuss reliability of the telephone system.

Five Nines means the system will be up and functioning for 99.999% of the time. It relates to uptime over a period of 365 days or 1 year.

Do you know how much time your system is allowed to be down, or out of service, to meet the requirement of Five Nines?

If a system were up only 99% of the time, also known as Two Nines, it would be out of service for 3 days, 15 hours, 40 minutes during a yearly period.

For Three Nines or 99.9%, it would be 8 hours, 46 minutes.

For Four Nines or 99.99%, it would be 52 minutes, 36 seconds.

And for Five Nines or 99.999%, drum role please. The total amount of outage over a one year period is 5 minutes, 15 seconds.

When looking at those numbers, it's obvious why they boast about Five Nines reliability.

Does your number mean anything?

Depending on what type of business that you are in may depend on what type of telephone number you have. If you are a business with most of your customers and clients located in your local area, you don't want to have a telephone number that is based in another town or over 100 miles away.

Before text messaging became the fad, the letters on the numbers of a telephone keypad weren't used much. But if you ask folks who had telephone number in the 40's and 50's those letters meant something. I'm sure you may have heard of something like Klondike 5-3825.

In the 80's and 90's there was a craze for vanity numbers. Do you recall the commercials featuring 1 800 CALL ATT.

I personally didn't like vanity numbers. It always seemed to take me 2 to 3 times longer to dial. I've never memorized the letters on the keypad and had to hunt to dial.

Once when I was involved with converting a company over to a new telephone system as well as a new exchange, we thought about vanity numbers. We did have the cafeteria's number end in FOOD, a friend of mine kept DICK and another DAVE. Can you guess their names?

We used some and others were reserved. It probably wasn't a good idea when we issued the chief executive 3932. He didn't want his private number easily known.

It was taking us too much time for us to complete the project on-time so we only went with some common ones. Those that came to mind quick or a person asked us if it was available. Maybe it was a good idea, since if we looked deeper we may not have issued some of the numbers to those we did.

Have you ever looked to see what your number spells? FOOD is 3663. Dick is 3425. Dave is 3283. Look around. You may be surprised what can be spelled from a telephone number.

Let's look at Klondike 5-3825 for example.

The letters for 3 are DEF, 8 are TUV, 2 are ABC and 5 are JKL. With those letters you can make Klondike 5-DUCK.

Can you see what else it spells? It's a word that is not commonly used in conversation, unless it's in a bedroom.

I don't think I would want to have the telephone number 382-5968 or 328-7448 either. You can figure those out.

Music on Hold - Is yours legal?

Music-on-hold (MoH) has been around so long that it has almost become a given that when you place a caller on hold they should hear something other than silence. If nothing else it gives the caller the sense that they haven't been disconnected while they wait.

Many businesses have MoH. It's easy to add to many telephone systems, simply plug a music source to the jack marked music. Believe it or not, many of the common sources that are plugged into that jack actually are not legal to use.

When the technician installed the telephone system, he may have asked if you wanted Music on Hold. You may not have even thought about it until the question was asked. The usual response is 'Yes, that's a good idea'.

Music on Hold, while being simple to add, the legal aspects are far from simple and need to be considered. Many technicians and sales persons aren't aware of the legal issues involved. They are just trying to satisfy their clients. The next thing you know you are being asked what radio station you want on it.

Radio stations are not legal to be put on MoH systems. There are copyright issues involved with the music played by the radio stations. They have the right to broadcast the music, but not the rebroadcast rights. When you put music from a radio onto your telephone system it's rebroadcasting the station.

What about Talk Radio? The radio station as well as the on-air talent has the rights of rebroadcast and unless you have gotten permission from them it can't be used.

Then next common source is digital music. This is a CD or MP3. This is just as illegal as the radio for many of the same reasons.

But you may be saying, I purchased the CD can't I use it as I please? When purchasing a CD you only own a copy of it, not the rights to the music on the CD.

The rights you do have are called private performance rights. When the music is put onto your on-hold system this is classified as a Public Performance. Songwriters, composers and publishers have under the copyright laws exclusive right of public performance and any public performance requires permission.

There are three music industry organizations where you can go to purchase rights for Music for on-hold. Those are ASCAP, BMI and SESAC. For a fee you can use music that these organization license for rebroadcast.

The information about music rights not only applies to Music on Hold, but also if you use background music in the office through a centralized system.

Many times you may have gotten something specially produced for your MoH that has advertising for your company. This is a good use for MoH, but when having this created you need to be certain that the producer has gotten the rights to all of their material.

There are also royalty-free sources of music, but the agreement should be check to be certain that it can be used in MoH systems.

What can happen? Many businesses may continue to use one of these sources long after they may have learned that they are not legal, thinking that they will never be caught. On that all I can say is that BMI is out there looking for businesses using unlicensed and have imposed fines of many of thousand of dollars.

Businesses can subscribe to music services such as "Music Choice", "DMX" or "Muzak". The music services have bulk buying agreements and they may be able to provide music for less than licensing with the music industry organizations.

Music on hold has many benefits. You just need to be aware and understand your legal rights in using it.

Adding or removing service.

Over the course of time, one thing that is almost certain, you will need to change telecommunication services. It may be that additional numbers or lines are ordered. Or services no longer needed are disconnected. There maybe just a simple change in features.

There are some things to remember when changing service. The actual addition or subtraction of the service may be easy, but the process may not be and could take many months.

You will rarely have the changes occur on the exact day that the billing period begins or end. Since most telecommunication services are paid for in advance, credits for disconnected services will be given. It could take a couple of invoices until all of the credits are received.

It's also not unusual for the service to be disconnected, but not removed from the invoice. There are also times that services may no longer being billed, but they are still being delivered to the service location.

While this may not seem like a problem, it could be. Later you may find that a disconnected line was needed and order a replacement. When installation is occurring it could be discovered there's not enough facilities for the service to be installed at your location. The records of the old service still show it's there. Or it may have been disconnected from your system, but later a technician repairing the system may mistakenly connect it. Now you are using it and a mysterious bill appears.

Here are some simple guidelines to follow when changes are made to telecommunication services.

- Request any change in writing. The initial request may be made via telephone, but the request should be followed in writing. Ask the process clerk for an address to send the written request. If following this route, be certain to add any existing ordering information so that the services are duplicated.

- Along with the order number, get the due date. Make sure to get the contact information of all persons who will be handling your order.

- If ordering a disconnect check a few days after the due date to verify that the service is disconnected and that the recording you receive is what's expected.

- Follow the billing path. Check for credits, if applicable, for disconnected services. If new services, check that billing begins when expected. Do not assume that it will appear on the bill, occasionally new services may not appear on the bill for a few months and when it does they are allowed to back bill.

Cell Phones

What do you need your cell phone to do?

When looking at the evolution of cell phones it's amazing to see what they have become. They have become the Swiss army knife of technology gadgets.

When I first got involved in cell phones they were called car phones. This was in the mid 1980's and the only practical place for it was in the car. There weren't many cell sites and the transmitting power of the cell phone was much greater than it is today. The energy required to transmit that power was much greater too.

The first portable phone was called a bag phone and in many cases it was simply a car phone that was packaged into a bag with a battery the size of a paperback book. Battery technology has changed a great deal since those days as well.

The principle use of a cell phone, then as well as now is to communicate from one person to another. The technology, or maybe just the marketability of the cell phone has cause it to become a multi-faceted device. One that is not only used to talk to an associate across town, or across county, but one that allows you to take pictures, keep your schedule, send text, email messages or listen to music.

Is this a good thing?

That depends on whom you ask. I personally would rather have multiple devices, each which is designed for a purpose. Usually the ones that are included in a cell phone will only partly deliver.

Cell phone cameras, while getting better with each new issue, still do not measure up to the quality of a digital camera. It's better than one purchased 4 years ago, but not as good as the new one. The resolution of the pictures isn't as good, nor does it have all of the features of the camera, such as zoom and flash. The only good thing I can see about a cell phone camera is the one purpose it shouldn't be used and that is taking unaware pictures.

The digital music players of cell phones are pretty similar, the only difference may be storage. But, aren't there times you may want to go somewhere, call it alone time, to listen to music and not be bothered with having a cell phone?

I thought at one time it was a good idea to have my calendar on my cell phone. Soon I discovered that it was harder to enter into it meetings nor did it have the same information as my PDA. I ended up carrying both anyway using the cell phone calendar less.

Cell phones now have many of these added features included, but I look at the phone and think, isn't that just a bit big to be lugging around when I want to go jogging.

Where do you need to be doing business?

Many companies, especially those dealing with defense contacts are requiring cell phones with cameras to be left at the security desk. This sure makes it hard to call someone to get additional information while in the meeting.

All of these are things to think about when you deciding on a new cell phone. Do you need one that has all the bells and whistles, some of which may or may not ever be used?

Some factors to consider when selecting a cell phone.

Plan Minutes: Too many and you are spending money for throwaway minutes. Too few and you may be paying a premium price for those few extra minutes.

Features: Don't pay for features you don't need. If you don't text message, then don't pay for a text-messaging plan. Most cell carriers have reasonable rates for texting if you are only using it a few times a month

Phone: Do you need a phone that has a camera, calendar or music player? If you aren't going to use it, you don't need it and those phone do cost a bit extra.

Do Not select the cell phone you want to use then go to the carrier that supplies it. It may not be the best carrier for your needs. Over the years I have been asked which is the best cell phone to get.

My answer has always been, decide on the carrier and then choose the phone.

The one thing to always remember about the cell phone, while acting like a telephone, it is actually a two-way radio. For it to work it needs to be within range of a cell tower that uses the same frequencies. Factors that can determine coverage include hills, trees and structures.

Having worked at a small college, I can assure you there's nothing worst to see than an irate 18 year old college freshman with a brand new cell phone, one with all the new and fancy features, that's nothing more than a paperweight since there's no signal from their carrier.

All Cell Phones are not created equal

You've just seen an advertisement showing the perfect cell phone for you. Now you are ready to run out and get it.

You have just fell into the trap that cell phone providers have developed. Since all phones cannot be used on all networks, they have gotten you to go to theirs.

Are you in one of these situations?
1) unhappy with your current cell phone and provider?
2) one of the rare first-time buyers?
3) relocating to another area or decided to look for a new phone?

It doesn't matter. The first thing to address is always the same. Look for the system that will supply you with the best service for the least cost.

All cellular networks are not created equal. Many factors are involved, including number of transmitting locations and channels they can support. It's not important to understand the technical just the reality.

How do you find the best carrier?

Ask! Ask your neighbors, co-workers, members of the church you attend, people at the places your regularity visit.

In a short period of time you will discover which carrier may or may not be working for them.

Only once you have determined the carrier you want to use, is it time to decide on the phone. One of the best things to do is to make a list of features you want. Are you looking for a smart-phone, one that is almost a mini-computer in your hands, or are you looking for one to take with you in case of emergencies? Do you need a camera? A music player?

Each carrier has a web page with phones. It gives description of the phones along with their features. This will help narrow it down.

It's probably a good idea to go to a phone store. Go to one that will allow you to hold a working one in your hands. You will want to use the buttons and see how the features work. If you enjoy using it, the experience will be enhanced.

You don't have to buy the phone at the store, it's possible that you may be able to find it less expensive on-line. But seeing and holding it in the store will give you an understanding on the weight, size and buttons of the phone.

Don't forget accessories. A car charger is a good idea as is having a headset. Do you need a carrying case or an extra battery or charger? Check these prices as well.

Evaluate the total cost. The plan, the phone, accessories and hidden cost such as contract cancellation penalties. By seeing the cost over the contract period, you'll have a good idea of the total expense for the phone and service.

What cell phone service plan is best?

It may seem too simplistic, but the answer is the one that works best for you. There are many factors to consider, but the most important may not be the cost.

Does it work in the locations where you need it to work? If most of your work is within a city, cost may be the most important factor, since most carriers work well within high population areas. What is a cell phone worth, if the location where you spend most of the day, you get that dreaded 'No Signal' icon?

Many businesses cringe when they open the invoice for their wireless service. It sometimes seems as if controlling those costs is a never ending game, but these quick items are things to look at to help control those cost.

- Are you paying replacement insurance? If you are should you? How many phones do you have? If you have a few, it's probably a good idea to have the insurance, accidents will happen. If you have quantity of phones, the added cost of the replacement plans may be greater than the costs of replacements over the contacted period.

- How are you using your minutes? Do you regularly use more minutes than you have on your plan. If you are, by increasing your plan minutes could save you a few dollars. It's also the case if you are not using your minutes. By decreasing your plan minutes you may save as well. Do you have a plan that you meet the minutes only once or twice a month?

- Are you paying for extras that aren't being used? Being able to make or receive a text message is great, but are you paying for a texting plan, but not using it. Most carriers have a reasonable rate for single messages. This also works the other way. Are you using a lot of text messages that are billed at message rates?

The only way to know for sure is to study your bills, or have an expert come in to review the invoices, and not just each month, but over a period of time. A year period is best. That length of time can give you trends on how the phones are being used.

Can I use my cell phone in my car?

Cell phones are a valuable way of conducting business, but at the same time they have raised a lot of issues involving safety. Some states have passed laws prohibiting talking on a cell phone while driving without using a hands free device. Those include the District of Columbia, New Jersey and New York. Some cities and counties may also have restrictions.

But doesn't it really depend on you? Do you feel comfortable driving while talking? If talking on the cell phone diverts your attention from driving, the best action could always be to pull to the side of the road and bring your conversation to an end. This also may be best if you are traveling in areas where cell phone coverage may not be at it's best. Stop at a location where you are getting a good signal and you won't be bothered with drop-outs.

There may also be liability issues. If an employee has an auto accident and harms someone while making a work-related cell phone call, the employer as well as the employee may be found liable.

Lawsuits have been filed around the nation and companies have settled before going to court. It's best to check with legal representation on the best policies to establish.

If one must use cell phone while in their cars, the following safety guidelines are useful:

- Know the features of the phone, such as speed dial and redial and how to use them.

- Dial the number while the car is not moving.

- Heavy traffic and bad weather is not a good time to be using the phone. Full attention should be on driving.

- Use speed dialing as much as possible.

- Use a hands-free phone.

- Do not look up phone numbers while driving.

- Stressful conversations should not be held while driving.

- Keep your eyes on the road.

- Do not take notes.

Whose number is it?

Businesses use a multitude of tools to get their work done. It doesn't matter whether you have a product or a service. All businesses have to sell. There are plenty of 'cost to do business' items to get this done.

Most businesses would never dream of allowing their employees to own or control important sales tools. But it seems as if some businesses have no problem in allowing their employees, especially those in sales, from controlling their cell phone number.

There are many reasons for this, such as the cost involved in administrating the accounts. It may be easier to give them a monthly expense for it, or even reimburse the entire bill. It may seem to the owner or manager of the business that they are doing the employee a favor by not forcing them to have a business and personal cell phone. Of course there are IRS issues involved with this. The IRS still consider cell phones to be a taxable fringe benefit. But that's not part of this conversation.

Is it wise or is it a big mistake to allow the employee that much control.

Is it a pure sales based company, reselling a product made by others? If you are, you probably require your salesperson to have a cell phone so they can always be in touch with your clients.

The salesperson may think it's their clients, but they really are yours. Do you control that cell phone number or your salesperson?

Salespersons will make many contacts and hand out even more business cards. The telephone number on the business card may have the desk number.

Salesmen like to be directly contacted and even though the cell phone may not be printed on the card, the client probably has been given the cell phone number?

What happens if the salesperson decides to leave your employ to work for your chief competitor? Your client dials the cell phone number of his favorite salesperson. An order is placed and instead of your company getting the business, your competitor has it and you've just lost a client.

It may be time to rethink the issue of whether you should consider the cell phone and its number as another asset that you own.

If you allow the employee to control their cell phone number, why don't you let them control their desk number?

Who knows, the number that you protect may be the one that is called in the middle of the night that could make, or break your business depending on whose salesperson is at the other end of that conversation.

Hello, I can't talk right now I'm at a funeral.

When it comes to talking on cell phone some people think it's their right to talk and use it wherever or whenever they please.

Most times if they would look around and think about where they are, whom they are with, or what is happening, they would think twice about using the phone. They may even wonder if having it turned on is proper.

For example one day I was standing at a graveyard ceremony during a funeral and my cell phone started ringing. Fortunately it was a ring, and not one of those musical ring tones.

I had thought I had turned it off before entering the funeral home, which is what I normally would have done. I obviously hadn't. The phone ringing at that place and time was one of my most embarrassing moments.

There needs to be some cell phone etiquette. There are places where the cell phone should be turned off. They don't need to be turned on when attending a funeral or going to church. Do you really need to have the cell phone ringing or vibrating while trying to woo a prospective client?

There are plenty of places where you should have the phone on vibrate. In my mind that is anytime that you aren't either in your own home, car or office. How many times have you been in a room of people and a cell phone starts ringing and everyone checks to see if it's theirs?

There are places where you really don't need to be talking on the phone. If you wouldn't want to hear someone on a phone, it's a place where others feel the same.

A movie theatre or even at a table in a restaurant is such a place. There's usually a lobby area where you can take an important call.

At times I wonder how important the call may be. It seems as if no one can make a decision on anything without picking up a cell phone and placing a call. "Honey, I'm at the grocery store and would you rather me get beans instead of tomatoes, the tomatoes don't look very good today."

Have you ever had the person next to you ask a question, as you start to answer you realize he asked the question to the person he's talking with on the cell phone? If you haven't, I'm surprised.

At least now if you walk down the street talking to yourself, everyone around you will just think you're talking on the cell phone.

Can Cell Phones cause fires at gas pumps?

There's an email circling the Internet reporting that the Shell Oil Company has issued a warning confirming incidents of cell phones causing fires at gas pumps. I wondered about this so I started to do a little research to see whether it was true.

At the end of the email it said for additional information I could to go to the Petroleum Equipment Institute web page www.pei.org/. So that was the first place I went. Interesting when I followed the directions, which said to go to STOP STATIC, although it's actually Safe Fueling, I found this statement at the top of the page. "Not Cell Phones - PEI has investigated hundreds of refueling fires and flare-ups. We have not documented one single incident that was caused by a cellular telephone."

But that doesn't mean there isn't a danger. The PEI further states; "The Petroleum Equipment Institute began investigating mysterious refueling fires in the mid-Nineties. We learned that static electricity – the same thing that shocks you after dragging your feet across the carpet – can ignite gasoline vapors at the pump."

In this computer age I went to the place where many people go for information, Google. I googled the words "Shell Oil Company cell phone fires". The first result to the inquiry was at www.snopes.com, a web site that researches Urban Legends.

At www.snopes.com/autos/hazards/gasvapor.asp it is reported that this urban legend is false. No one can find any records that Shell Oil issued any warning and no proof has ever been shown that cell phone can cause gas pump fires.

While one part of the email is false, it is a fact that gas fires do occur. They are caused not by cell phones but by static.

Since static has been verified as a possible cause to fuel fires at gas pumps, the PEI has issued these guidelines on fueling your vehicle:

- Turn off your vehicle engine. Put your vehicle in park and/or set the emergency brake. Disable or turn off any auxiliary sources of ignition such as a camper or trailer heater, cooking units, or pilot lights.

- Do not smoke, light matches or lighters while refueling at the pump or when using gasoline anywhere else.

- Use only the refueling latch provided on the gasoline dispenser nozzle. Never jam the refueling latch on the nozzle open.

- Do not re-enter your vehicle during refueling. If you cannot avoid re-entering your vehicle, discharge any static build-up BEFORE reaching for the nozzle by touching something metal with a bare hand -- such as the vehicle door -- away from the nozzle.

- In the unlikely event a static-caused fire occurs when refueling, leave the nozzle in the fill pipe and back away from the vehicle. Notify the station attendant immediately.

Do I use the cell phone when I'm refueling? On the PEI site there is a clip showing a fire caused by static. That clip has made me aware of dangers at the gas pumps. With all of the usual distractions I can understand why accidents occur.

Haven't we all heard of someone driving away with the fueling nozzle still in the car? I think this is one of those places where cell phone conversations can wait. But as always it's up to you to make the final decision.

Cell Phone users shouldn't talk during a storm.

Believe it or not, several people have been struck by lightning around the world, while talking on their cell phone. A few countries are now recommending that people do not talk on their phones outside during a lightning storm.

Many people do not realize that their cell phone is a metallic object. Also lightning will tend to go to a point, such as a cell phone antenna.

When lightning strikes a cell phone it disrupts the effect known as a flashover. This is a phenomenon where the electricity passes around the body and does less damage.

However, holding a metallic object or cell phone disrupts the flash over effect and allows all that magnificent energy to target internal organs

Not to mention, it's unwise to increase your odds of getting struck in the first place by talking on a live radio with an antenna in a lightning storm.

There are also stories of people being struck by lightning while talking on their home or office telephone. When considering the fact that the process of a telephone conversation is to move electronic impulses from one point to another over a wire, it would be logical to think that lightning could also transverse that wire.

A cordless telephone may be safer, but it uses the same principles as the cell phone. It just may be safer to read a book during the storm.

Is there a Cell Phone Directory?

Every few months I will either receive or be handed an email with the announcement that cell phone numbers will be released to telemarketers or that they will be released into a cell phone directory.

While there are some who would enjoy that possibly of cell phones being part of a directory, at this point that idea is nothing more than an email floating around and upsetting some users.

A few years ago there was a movement to create a cell phone directory. While many of the cellular carriers were in favor of this, VerizonWireless from the beginning was against the practice. With concerns from the public being raised to their governmental legislators and the lack of support from a couple of the major carriers that idea died.

Even if a cell phone directory does happen, it is not planned for anytime soon. Also the cellular industry is concerned about preserving the privacy of the users and having a listing in a cell phone directory would require the user to approve its insertion.

There are a number of reasons that cell phone customers are opposed to a Wireless 411:

- They prefer their privacy and want to know that their cell phone numbers are available only to those to whom they provide them. They don't want other people being able to obtain their cell phone numbers without their consent or knowledge.

- They are concerned that their cell phone numbers will be sold to telemarketers.

- They see one of the goals of the Wireless 411 service as a ploy to spread cell phone numbers to wider circles of friends and acquaintances, who will then place calls to cell phones and thereby force cell customers to pay for additional wireless minutes.

The wireless companies behind the proposed Wireless 411 service contend that their service will be beneficial to cellular customers and that they have addressed those customers' major concerns:

- The service would save money for the millions of customers who have cellular phones and currently pay to have their cell phone numbers listed in phone directories.

- The Wireless 411 service will be included in the directory only if they specifically request to be added and there is no charge for requesting to be included or choosing not to be included.

- The Wireless 411 information will not be published in a book or on the Internet. It would be made available only to operator service centers performing the 411 directory assistance service.

Even if a directory were established it would not open up telemarketer to be able to call cell phones. It is illegal for marketers who use an auto-dialer, very few do not, to call wireless telephone numbers.

Some versions of the email state that cell phone users need to add their number to the national Do-Not-Call Registry and erroneously state there is a specific deadline for getting listed.

Since its inception the DNC list has allowed people to add their cell phone numbers and there has never been a deadline. There is not a separate list for cell phones.

Telephone numbers can be added to the list at anytime by either calling a toll-free registration number from the telephone to be added or using the on-line form. Once entered it remains on the list for five years. The list was started in 2003.

Business numbers cannot be entered into the Do-Not-Call list. The list does not prohibit marketing to businesses by other businesses.

Entering yours or the boss's number to the Do-Not-Call list will not prevent a marketer from calling, nor would you have any lawful recourse against them.

VoIP

A New Telephone System?

Many titles went through my mind while determining a title for this article. One was 'Do you need a new telephone system?' Another was; 'What type of telephone system do I need?' A third thinking about VoIP was; 'Do I need to change my telephone system to VoIP?'

I decided on the title 'A New Telephone System?' Why? I felt that information was needed describing a telephone system and what a telephone system is before asking any of those questions. It is for that reason I put this as the first tip in the VoIP section.

What is a telephone system? A telephone system is comprised of several items. There is the telephone control unit, often hidden in a closet. Then there's the wiring. The item most often considered the telephone is the telephone set that sits on the desk. In VoIP the telephone may be software that resides on your computer.

The set is often the part that makes or breaks a telephone system. It may be the least important part of the system. The telephone set is what the user associates with the telephone. If the user is not happy with the telephone set, it really doesn't matter how well engineered the system may be, it will always be thought as lousy.

There are many factors to consider when making the decision on a new telephone system.

You don't want to under invest in it. If people call your business and they feel that the telephone call is bad or amateurish, they may decide not to do business with you. Are their calls routed incorrectly? Do they receive busies? Are they faced with automated options that are confusing? Invest the time and the resources to do it right.

Consider the existing telephone assets. Is your present system relatively new? Parts of it may be reused or integrated into a new system. Some VoIP systems can be designed as integrated telephone systems.

Decide what features you need and want. Create a list and prioritize those features. Some common features are call forwarding and transfer, call detail recording, voice mail and music-on-hold. Use the list to help assist in evaluation of the total system cost.

It's important to have trust in the telephone vendors and consultants that you contract. Someone will need to install, configure and maintain the system.

When selecting a vendor be certain to get references from them. When requesting a reference list, don't be afraid to ask for a list of customers not just those on the top of their reference list. All vendors have customers who love them and others who are neutral to them. By getting comments from a wide customer base, you can have a good view on their service.

You may want to consider a lease instead of purchase. Leasing could increase the total cost of a telephone system, but it also allows you to have a known monthly expenditure.

Selecting the time to purchase a telephone system may help determine the price paid. Some sales reps may have quarterly quotas to reach. It's possible to get a better deal at the end of those quarters than at the beginning.

When considering a telephone system, you may also need to be review the wiring in the office. If replacing a traditional telephone system with a VoIP system, you may also be required to replace the wiring. This could increase the cost of the system greatly.

When determining the cost of a telephone system there is a couple of things to keep in mind. These costs include:

- Telephone system hardware.

- Installation including additional wiring if required.

- Determine the charge for changes needed during the first month after installation and when those changes are made. It's a common practice for vendors to allow one visit at the end of the first month to make changes. If you can't wait they may charge for an earlier visit.

- Staff Training. It's a good idea to trade the staff prior to the change and have someone available during the first few hours of use.

- Warranty period. A year is a common period, but some may be less, other more.

- Maintenance cost after warranty period ends. It's a good idea to plan out a five year total cost.

When should a telephone system be replaced? Others may disagree but I have concluded that these are the only reasons to replace a telephone system:

- The company has outgrown the present system. There may not be any expansion paths, or those that are available may not be cost effective.

- Due to poor maintenance or lack of performing upgrades, the current system would cost more to maintain and/or upgrade than to replace.

- Due to an outside influence, you or your management declares that the system is obsolete and that the best course is to move to new technology.

How does VoIP work?

The Internet has established many new things. Companies no longer have to send printed catalogs to customers. These can be placed on-line at websites. One of the biggest advantages to this is that it can never be out of date. Products can be added or removed as needed along with any price changes.

With this technology another new product is on the market. That is Voice over Internet Protocol or VoIP. But what is VoIP?

To understand VoIP there's a need to understand traditional telephony. The telephony standard uses what is termed circuit switched technology. When a circuit switched telephone call is made there is a direct and dedicated path from one caller to another. This path is reserved for the entire conversation.

You may have seen in old movies an executive in California asking his secretary to place a call to New York. Then 15 minutes later he is told that the call is ready. What happened during that time wasn't waiting for the party on the other end to get to the call, but waiting for the telephone company to connect a circuit between the two locations. That's one of the reasons why long distance calls were so expensive.

VoIP treats the voice as data. This technology turns the voice into tiny digital packets of information. Those packets are transmitted over the data network. When received at the other end, the data is returned to audio that can be heard.

Voice IP is not the same as Data IP. In Data communications, such as sending an email, the data may go to a server to be compiled before delivering to the user. Even if it's from one computer to another the data packets are received and assembled. If one packet happens to be missing or is corrupted there is a request to resend it.

Voice is a real time event. IP Packets are assembled as they are received. Packets received out of sequence are not used. Because of this, there could be missing or delayed information. In technical terms, latency and jitter. To the ear it may be choppy or unusable speech.

VoIP and Regulations

One of the reasons that VoIP would appear to be less expensive than traditional telephony is the absence of some regulatory fees and taxes.

Usually with telecommunication services the federal government gives the States the right to regulate through their Public Service Commissions.

Because of a definition in the Telecom Act of '96, the controlling body of the Federal Government, the Federal Communications Commission (FCC) and federal courts has determined that VoIP cannot be regulated by the states. The FCC has decided, with some exceptions, not to regulate VoIP.

One ruling that the FCC has made deals with 911. In the ruling the providers of interconnected VoIP services (interconnected refers to the ability to receive call from or terminate calls to the Public Switched telephone network) must supply 911 capabilities to their customers. The FCC understands that the service may not be exactly like the traditional 911 services and there may be limitations.

Another of the FCC ruling is that VoIP providers are required to pay into the Universal Service Fund (USF). The fund was created by the Telecom Act of '96 to subsidize telecommunications services in rural and other high-cost areas such as schools and libraries. USF charges do not have to be passed directly to the customer, some VoIP providers may not impose those fees, but many will.

Because of these two requirements VoIP have to increase their charge for services.

As the States and the federal government decide the final outcome on who shall be regulate or in some case what shall be regulated, it's important to know and understand, what is true today about VoIP fees and taxes may change in the near future.

Is VoIP the right fit for Small Businesses?

VoIP is similar to any technology in that it needs to fit into the business plan. Deciding if it fits will be determined by a number of items.

If you are one that wants to be first in line to use any new technology, you will move toward using it. There are others who won't adapt or migrate until everything is perfect. Since rarely is everything perfect, they will always have an excuse.

Others will wait until it fits their business and technology plans. It will be seen as a need option or as a replacement for their present telephone system.

VoIP has been proclaimed the service to move your telephone needs if you want to save money. But that **May Not** be true. To believe it without doing research will probably lead to a disappointment. At worst it could make you look like a fool.

If your company has multiple locations, especially if they are not in the same local calling area, or has employees that are telecommuting, VoIP may be right for you.

VoIP calls between remote offices usually cost nothing, and equipping telecommuters using traditional technology can be costly.

If you are in the process of wiring for a new office, VoIP may also make sense. Wiring for one common system, Voice and Data, is less expensive than wiring for both.

The best solution may be to use the existing telephone system in the office and use VoIP for the calls between offices or to the public.

Even if you are using the traditional telephone network, you still may have been using IP without realizing it. Telecommunication carriers have used IP in their networks for some time.

Will IP telephony be the way of the future? With the speed that technology changes, nothing is for certain. Tomorrow someone may develop a technology that makes VoIP look as ancient as the circuit switched network.

Many business owner will continue to think if it ain't broke, don't fix it. If it works don't replace it.

Many traditional telephone systems have been installed over the years that won't be replaced until they simply don't work anymore.

Benefits and Drawbacks of VoIP

Have you ever wondered what some of the benefits of VoIP are? Or the disadvantages? The following will give some advantages and drawbacks of using VoIP.

Benefits:
Offices with multiple locations can have a common office telephone system that is less expensive than traditional telephony technology. There can be seamless call transfers, easier collaboration due to extension dialing and calls between offices over great distance are free.

VoIP systems, since they are part of the data network infrastructure, may be easier to manage. There is only one network instead of two. There would be separate telephone hardware to maintain, but the management is of one central network.

The Move, Add and Change (MAC) process is simplified. Since the intelligence is in the telephone the person 'on the go' may be able to plug their telephone into any Internet connection to use the same phone they are use to in the office. If they are using a 'soft phone' a telephone that resides on a computer, they have their phone and data in one place.

Drawbacks:

VoIP put a huge demand on the computer network. The data network has been use to being what some define as a 'messy network'. This means data packets could arrive out of order or lost needing to be resent, then reconstituted before use. Voice conversations will sound distorted or choppy if the packets do not arrive in the correct order or are lost. Procedures need to be established that allows VoIP traffic to have a higher priority throughout the entire network than data traffic.

VoIP systems require more attention. When updating software on servers or network switches, assurances has to be made that those changes will not cause problems with the voice traffic.

When telephone service is absolutely critical, the complete network needs to be designed to prevent outages. These outages could be as simple as a power failure. Power backups and redundant plans need to be established and implemented.

Fax machines may or may not work with VoIP. To use a Fax machine an adapter would be required. With a Fax machine, packets that are lost and not noticeable to the ear may prevent the Fax from successfully being received.

VoIP and IP security?

A VoIP system since it uses the same technology face the same type of problems as the data network. This includes VoIP versions of spam, phishing, and denial of service attacks.

These attacks could take down the network and telephone system for hours. Calls could be intercepted divulging company secrets or client information.

The threats to a VoIP system are some of the same ones that affect any IP network. Others are unique to voice communications. Major threats include:

- A virus or worm can be introduced to the network and crash the VoIP servers or gateways

- A denial of service attack can overwhelm the network, making it unusable

- A hacker can access the call server to listen in to, record, or disrupt calls

- A hacker can get access to services that are supposed to be restricted

- Hackers can access the trunk gateway to the PSTN and make unauthorized toll calls

- A hacker who accesses the call server can register "rogue" IP phones, which can then use the company's VoIP services

A related problem is VoIP spam or VoIP Phishing. A replicated voice messages could be created that could be used for purposes, such as obtaining personal information. People trust the telephone more than a do with a computer and email and are more likely to offer important information on the phone.

Does this mean you shouldn't consider VoIP or move to it? There are cases where money can be saved by using VoIP.

What should be done is plan and prepare the network.

- Secure the VoIP servers. Mission critical servers, whether Voice or Data need to be secured against both internal and external intruders.

- Encrypt VoIP communications. A strong encryption scheme would render the information unusable if intercepted by a hacker.

- Redundancy for fault tolerance. This could mean multiple Internet connections and/or providers and clustered VoIP servers so that one automatically takes over if the other goes down.

Deploying VoIP without looking at the security concerns could be cause a major problem within your business with costly outages.

Misconceptions about VoIP

When talking with people about VoIP, it's not hard to discover that there are many misconceptions about it. The following are a few I've seen.

VoIP can save money. This may be true if you are making a great deal of long distance and international telephone calls. These calls through the traditional telephone network could have a high per minute cost. If your calls are to local users or those on your system, VoIP has little to no savings on calls. I've heard it said that VoIP calls are free. If it's from one VoIP user to another it may be. Some VoIP providers are now charging a monthly fee for calling the PSTN.

The computer needs to be on to use VoIP. This would depend on what type of VoIP telephone you are using. If you are using a soft-phone that resides on the computer that is true. If you have a VoIP adapter, the calls do not go through your computer. The adapter is another device on the network. The call will probably still be going through a VoIP server. The server may be on your premises and that would need to always be on. But to an average user, it would be no different that the central telephone unit that usually buried in a closet.

VoIP cannot be used in conjunction with your present telephones. Even in larger businesses a combined traditional, VoIP solution is usually the best. Fax machines will require the use of a VoIP adapter, which can also be used with any normal telephone. If using a PBX or Key system digital phone system, VoIP can be used to connect to the Public Network.

You can keep your present telephone number. This may or may not be true. There are many factors involved in porting a telephone number from one type of service to another. While it may be able to happen, many times it may not be easy or smooth.

Any Internet connection will work. Don't expect VoIP to work over a dial-up connection. Even connections in hotels or public WiFi spots may not be configured with enough bandwidth to carry all of the IP traffic, voice and data, that may be carried on it. In the office a DSL or Cable connection may not have the bandwidth required depending on the number of users on the telephone at the same time.

Questions when considering VoIP

It may at first seem natural to move to VoIP. It seems as if everyone is saying it's the way to go. But there are some things to consider before making the move.

1) How robust is your network? With VoIP network traffic will be increased. Both the internal network, also term Intranet and the external network need to be addressed. If you are experiencing slow time with your present network, to move to VoIP it will need to be upgraded as well. Your Intranet needs to have modern data switches and not older hubs.

2) What is the speed of your connection to the Internet? Many small businesses use DSL or Cable Modems to connect to the Internet. While these services are idea for normal Internet traffic VoIP may require more bandwidth.

3) How are you going to power the phones? Many telephone systems deliver power to the telephone sets via the cable from the control unit. VoIP services may not do this. Telephones may need to be powered by bulky transformers at the desk. VoIP telephones can be powered through the cabling plan, but unless the existing data switches have Power Over Ethernet

(POE) you will either have to purchase new Ethernet switches or live with the bulky transformers.

4) What are the plans for power failure? Older telephone systems may have battery backup on the central unit so that during power failures the telephones will continue to work. In VoIP systems you need to be sure that the power to the telephone set as well as the network equipment.

5) What telephone number will you get? Is it important for you business to have a local number? Some providers may not be able to offer to you a local telephone number. They also may not be able to transfer your current telephone number to their service.

6) Will you be paying for unused services? Do you have a maintenance contract on your present system? Do you have a contract for services from a telecommunications carrier? How long will it be until it ends? Can you cancel service without penalties?

Asking these questions as part of the decision making process will help make the transition easy if it's decided to move to VoIP.

It's a good idea to test the service before finalizing the process. If a vendor can't make a test telephone work to your satisfaction, they probably won't be able to install a complete system that will satisfy.

My recommendation to anyone, whether it's a small to mid-size business, or one that is classified as an Enterprise business is this simple approach.

Plan, Evaluate, Plan, Test, Plan, Implement.

Many of the people I've talked with who have installed VoIP solutions have said they should have spent more time planning.

Planning is an important consideration in any project, but it seems that with technology, and especially VoIP, the better the plan, the better the success.

Security

Inventory Control–Do you know what you have?

Over time it's amazing to see how much technology equipment a business can obtain. Do you know everything that you have? Do you know how old it is? Do you have a maintenance contract on something you took out of service months ago? These are all valid question, and some of you may be surprised with your answers.

Here are some ways to help control your inventory.

Start a database now, if you don't already have one. Whenever something is purchased, is the best time to enter the information into it.

Helpful information to keep in the database is the item description, serial number, cost, date of purchase, place of purchase and ending warranty date. I also keep an estimated useful life and have a column to enter the disposal date. I'm sure there are other items to put into it. There can be as much data as you deem necessary, but this is a good start. It only takes a few minutes to add the item.

Once you have the database started comes the hard part. It's not really hard, it's just time consuming. Enter all existing useful equipment into the database. If it's not useful throw it away.

Now here comes the real hard part. Put contracts for services into it. This includes maintenance contracts on equipment such as copiers, computers or telephone equipment. It should include the monthly service charges for telecommunication items such as telephone service (office and cellular), Internet service and all costs associated with them.

You may need to get your carrier involved to get updated information. The local phone company should be able to give you a CSR (Customer Service Record) that has detailed information on services they bill you.

The Internet carrier can provide the same. Be certain that you get details on speed of the connection. Most Internet connection has both an upload and download bandwidth value. Both are needed. This is the only way to be certain that the price being paid is competitive.

Make sure that you have all circuit ID's. These ID are what the service provider will need whenever a repair is requested. Often the main telephone number is thought to be the circuit ID, but that is simply the billing number. Having the correct circuit ID will speed repairs when they are needed.

Now that everything is in an organized location an informed technology decisions can be made without having to reinvent the wheel.

Is your network diagramed?

Most businesses no matter the size will usually have an organizational chart. With this chart it is helpful to evaluate performance as well as have a clear 'chain-of-operations'.

Do you have charts for your networks? Most business will have two networks in place, the telephone system and the data network. Having diagrams of those systems will be a real value whenever repairs are needed.

What type of information is important to keep on these diagrams? It's important to know the telecommunication services that are being used, as well as knowing where they are located.

Let's discuss the telephone system first. Are you using a multi-line telephone system? In most cases the answer is Yes. What type? That needs to be part of the chart. It's also important to know the location of the equipment associated with the system. Some systems may also have what's termed a Master Phone. Is that documented?

Now to address the data network. This network could be more complex and harder to figure out then the telephone system when repairs are needed and therefore more costly to repair without a network diagram. Information needed for this chart include location information, access speeds, port sizes and machine port addresses.

Whenever you have a new system installed or an existing one modified network drawing should be provided as part of the services. Unless you request or make this part of the service, it may not be done.

The biggest benefit to having network diagram is the time that will be saved. If your service provider needs to research information about your system to perform a repair, you are paying for his time. With up-to-date diagrams and information, it's easier to delegate repair responsibilities to the correct organization.

Present day copiers can be put onto a data network. If your copier breaks and they need to replace it, information is needed about the network to place the new one onto the system. With documentation you won't have to call your network service provider to get the information and access to the copier is provided quicker.

If you don't have the diagrams, you can have someone prepare them for you. You could wait until a repair is needed. But do you really want to have your telephones or data network out of service, while this is being done?

I would imagine it could put a big crimp on the day's bottom line while the telephone system or computer network is not working and time is being spent diagramming the system.

The telephone system and many pieces of the network equipment may have passwords. Do you know them? Or are they only known by your service provider?

You should have a copy of the passwords. They should be kept in a secure safe place until needed.

Now that you have the documentation just as important is having your staff know where the diagrams are stored? Not knowing where to locate them when needed is just like not having them at all.

Would you be ready for a software audit?

Computers have enabled us to do business quicker and in many cases easier. But the computer is nothing more than a box with a screen. You have to have the software programs to make the computer a productive tool.

Do you know all of the software that resides on your computer?

If you don't know it's probably time to find out. Software companies makes their living with software and they don't want their valuable commodity being used by companies who don't have the legal rights to use it. You need to know whether your software is in compliance with its Terms of Agreement.

There are many reasons that the software on the computers at your company may be out of compliance. Some companies may sell you the software for a limited amount of time. That time has lapsed and you are still using the software. You may have purchased the original software, but not the upgrade that one of your employees installed because they obtained it.

There may be cases where the software on your machine was purchased out of compliance for its use. Some software publishers will offer a discount, even allow for free use, if for personal use. These versions, while identical to the full version, will state in the user agreement that it is not allowed for commercial use. Using them for business purposes would make the software out of compliance.

You may not even be aware that the software is not in compliance. If you happen to fall under an audit it could cause a lot of trouble. Just the audit itself is troublesome; time is spent researching purchasing records, license agreement and other documents. After the audit you may find yourself in compliance, but most may find themselves out of compliance with little leverage in negotiations.

Here are some things to assist you with your software inventory.

- Have a computer policy. State how the computer should be used, who may install software and that software can only be installed once authorized.

- Have one person or team be the authorizing point.

- Document all software installed on every computer. Be certain that each copy has its own license.

- It's not a bad idea to once a year perform your own computer audit.

If an audit is performed you can with confidence give the auditor the documented software list for each machine.

How important are your contacts?

For many their lifeblood is based on their contacts and their telephone numbers. Where do you have those numbers stored? If it's only on your cell phone it's probably a good idea to back-up those numbers.

Cell phones are often the most replaced electronic item for a business. There are a number of reasons for it; among them are New Features that one feels is valuable and a lost or damaged phone.

It's handy to know that it's not impossible to quickly move those 200+ contacts on your present phone to a new one. There are software packages and services that can do it. Time is valuable and manually entering those contacts takes time.

There is always the fact that many of those old contacts are just not good any more. Losing them may not be a big deal. Only you can make that choice.

10 things to help secure your data

1) Back up early and often - Do it, as you are working as well as the end of the day.

2) Use file-level and share-level security - This helps keeps others away from your data.

3) Password-protect documents - Many programs allow this, but while it may be at times easy to crack, idle eyes won't have the time to do it.

4) Use EFS encryption - EFS uses a combination of asymmetric and symmetric encryption, for both security and performance. To encrypt files with EFS, a user must have an EFS certificate, which can be issued by a Windows certification authority or self-signed if there is no CA on the network.

5) Use disk encryption - Whole disk encryption locks the entire disk, but can be transparent to the user, once the password is entered. Always use this on removable disks.

6) Make use of a public key infrastructure - A public key infrastructure (PKI) is a system for managing public/private key pairs and digital certificates.

7) Hide data with steganography - You can use a steganography program to hide data inside other data. Example: hide a text file inside a graphic or music file.

8) Protect data in transit with IP security - Your data can be captured while it's traveling over the network by a hacker with sniffer software (also called network monitoring or protocol analysis software).

9) Secure wireless transmissions - Data that you send over wireless is more subject to interception than that sent over a wired Ethernet network.

10) Use rights management to retain control - You can use Windows Rights Management Services (RMS) to control what the recipients are able to do with the data they receive.

Are you your laptop's weakest link?

It's been in the news lately. A data analyst in the VA Administration, decided to take a laptop computer home to do some work. The idea was supposedly to save taxpayers money. The residence was burglarized. The laptop was stolen, along with all of the data stored on the computer.

What's surprising isn't that it happened. It's more surprising that it hasn't happened before now. Or worst it's been happening for years, but the fact hasn't reached the public ear.

Here's a question for you to think about. Can you afford to lose your laptop?

The laptop can be easily replaced, but what about the data? Has it been backed up? Does it hold information critical to your business? Does it hold an idea that is just about ready to be sent to the patent office?

What do you do? You could store your laptop computer in a bank vault? But you sure wouldn't get much work done on the road. One idea is to only carry the data that you need to do the day's or week's work, if you are traveling. Also not a good idea if you use a laptop as your only computer.

It is a good idea to encrypt sensitive information, with strong password protection. This includes your login password.

No matter what you do, there's always a risk of thief. If you make certain your laptop is secure when not with you it helps to prevent it. Lock it in the trunk when you are at a meeting. Double-check that your vehicle is locked.

There are times, possibly when traveling and staying in a hotel it doesn't make sense to take the computer with you. You can leave it in the room, but make certain it is secure. Many people have access into hotel rooms. It's also possible that the maid may be cleaning the bathroom leaving the door open for access to her cleaning cart, a thief could walk in; pretend to be the occupant and removes the laptop from the desk.

You could put it in the hotel safe. Or you could invest in a security cable and lock. Most laptop computers have a security slot that you can attach a cable or locking device. Wrap the cable around a heavy or stationary object, just like a bicycle.

Sometimes it's the usual things that you do, that could make for a very depressing time.

Does someone know more about you than you do?

It's scary. It seems as if just about everyday we are hearing about someone or some organization losing data about us.

But the real scary part is that these reports aren't about lost or thief that just happened, but ones that happened many months ago.

Your personal information may be in someone hands. Computers are stolen everyday. Many will be sold either as is or for parts. If lucky, it'll be with the data erased.

Having personal information fall into the wrong hands many times occurred due to poor management decisions. A database with critical personal information should never be put onto any type of portable device. Parts of that database, possibly, but not information such as Social Security number or other tax ID numbers.

How can you the small business owner protect the information of your clients?

- Create a firm data protection policy and within it create performance punishments. These could be suspensions, or terminations.

- Be certain that all of your employees know the policy and follow it. It's important they understand the reasons for the policy. Policies are always set up for a reason and all employees need to be educated on the reason.

- Don't be afraid to deal firmly with those that do don't adhere to the policy.

- And most of all, top management needs to follow the policy.

If you for some reason must have the personal data of clients on portable devices, the data needs to be well encrypted. Data encryption while putting a layer of startup in dealing with the data, in the long run may be the best time that you've ever spent.

Protect yourself from Identity Theft

It's bad enough that at times companies we do business may compromise our personal data, but what is worst, sometimes we are the ones that does the damage to ourselves. There are things you can do to help protect yourself wherever you may be.

At Home

Keep your personal information safe. Don't carry your social security number on your person or store it on your computer. Wallets are stolen all of the time and we all know of the dangers of computer viruses and other Trojan horses. You also don't want to have PIN (Personal Identification Number) near your checkbook or ATM cards.

Shred papers that may have confidential information. This includes applications for credit cards that may come to you in the mail.

Be aware of any emails, telephone calls or Internet requests for information. Unless you start the contact do not give out information such as credit card numbers, social security number, PIN's or birthdates. A common security measure for years has been your mother's maiden name. Protect that as well.

Check bank and credit card statements as soon as you receive them for any unexplained activity.

Check your credit reports at least once a year or whenever it is suspected there may be a problem.

Out of the house

Do not put information such as drivers' license numbers on credit card receipts. Take copies with you to shred at home.

Your social security number is needed by very few businesses. Always ask for the reason they need it and be certain you understand their reason before giving it. If they refuse to do business with you without that information, maybe it's best that you don't do business with them.

One of the newest trends is identity thief at the work place. Find out the policy about how your employer protects its employees and that data is stored securely. Also find out who may have access to your personal information.

What do you do if you think you have become a victim?

Contact the police to file a report. This does two things, one is to start an investigation and the second is you may need the police report to help straighten things.

Stop the damage. Contact the three credit bureaus, credit card companies and banks to inform them.

Gone Phishing! How not to get caught!

The Internet and email has made it easy to do things that were once hard. Such things as updating information to Credit Card companies once required a telephone call or a letter to make address changes and other updates.

Now you can do banking and check balances by signing into the bank's or Credit Card website and do those things.

While it has made some things easy it has also developed a bad side to the web as well. A practice call phishing is now running rampant through the Internet.

Phishing is characterized by attempts to fraudulently acquire information, such as passwords, Social Security numbers and other personal details, by masquerading as a trustworthy person or business in an apparently official electronic communication. The term phishing derives from the term password harvesting.

Legitimate email messages from companies to their customers will usually contain an item of information that is not readily available to phishers. Companies such as eBay and PayPal, always address their customers by their username in emails.

If an email addresses a user in a generic fashion ("Dear valued eBay member") it is likely an attempt at phishing.

Banks and credit card companies will often say something like "This message is about your account number XXXXXXXX1234" with all but the last few digits replaced by an "X" for security reasons.

It's always best to be suspicious if the message does not contain some specific personal information.

I've seen many messages; especially those that look like valid messages from PayPal and Ebay that have stated that my account has been put on hold and to reestablish the account click on a link and follow the questions asked. Closer look at the message showed it didn't have the personal information.

What do I do when I get one of these type messages? I use many different emails accounts. My first question, "Is this the email account I registered?" If it's not, then it's obviously a phishing attempt.

If it comes on the account that I did use to register, I never use the hyper-link to go to that account. I log on as usual. If the account needed information or had been put on hold, it would tell you. I have even had the same message being delivered to multiple accounts.

It's always best to be safe than sorry. It's advisable to never use a hyper-link from an email.

There have also been reports of a new type of phishing scheme. This involves receiving an email from a Bank or some other service that asks you to call a 1800 number rather than going to a fraudulent website.

Users are accustomed to calling 1800 numbers to request services and don't realize that toll free numbers can be registered with fake names and contact information.

When calling the number, the user is greeted by a message apparently from the bank, asked to enter the bank credit card number, expiration date, card holder social security number.

I stated that I use many email accounts. I recommend having at least three separate accounts. One is the work account and it should only be used for work related emails or personal emails from business contacts.

Another should be used as a personal account. This is the one that friends and relatives use for messages to you.

For the third account, use this as a junk account. This is the one that you enter into websites that require a valid email address.

Caution that bill may be only an advertisement.

The practice is not new. There are domain-registering companies who routinely send out a document to the domain name owner that appears as a bill to reregister your web name.

It is their way of having you transfer the registration of your web address from your current register to them. In some ways this may not be a bad thing, because at least it'll give you an idea when your domain name needs to be renewed.

If you don't remember, or you don't know because someone else set up the registration and that person is no longer associated with you, that's just sloppy record keeping.

It wouldn't surprise me that this may be more common than not. Domain names can be registered from one to five years and the person that set it up may have left long ago.

Questions to ask?

Do you know what names are registered? Have you just registered as .com? Did you also register as .net and/or .org?

It's best to register all that are available to you. If not someone else may have registered one of those and are using you to drum up business for themselves.

Do you know when your registration expires? Once it expires, it's free to be registered by another party. That would cause problems.

Do you know with which domain-registering company you originally registered the domain? If you do then you'd know that the document that looks like a bill is nothing more than, what it is, an advertisement.

This is just another of those things that can, but shouldn't, fall into an unknown crack in how you do business.

This is not the only type of misleading advertising you need to be aware. Recently I've received a check. Upon reading the information with it, I discovered that if I had deposited the check, I would be authorizing them to make monthly deductions for a service I had no desire to receive.

I guess there is some truth to the phrase, 'Buyer Beware'.

Wireless Communications Privacy

With each and everyday the use of wireless devices is growing. Many of us use a cordless telephone or a cell phone everyday. We even use wireless connections from our laptop computer to reach the Internet.

Have you ever considered how private the use of those devices may be? Is someone able to listen or intercept our messages?

Cordless phones can be intercepted and heard by others. In truth it may only be overheard briefly and accidentally. Devices such as baby monitors and other cordless phones may be able to pick up the signals. There are also scanners, the same ones that are used by people to listen to Fire or Police channels, that can pick up the frequencies. These scanners can pick up any frequency that is in their band.

Baby monitors, and home intercoms are other commonly used gadgets that are transmitting signals that others can receive. Cordless phones and scanners can pickup their signals as can the ones that your next-door neighbor may have.

Wireless microphones and wireless camera can also be intercepted. Wireless cameras are able to send a signal to a receiver so it can be viewed on a computer or TV and many homes and some offices are adding these as security systems. They may be far from secure. While they are inexpensive and relatively easy to install, they are also easy to monitor by voyeurs nearby who are using the same devices.

Cell phones have become a staple of communications, but you have to remember that these devices too are broadcast devices. It's not as bad as it was when all phones were analog, but the signals can still be picked up. Some phones will even convert to analog mode when digital services aren't available.

Some people seem to forget that when talking on the cell phone their end of the conversation can be heard by anyone standing close enough to hear. Many will use it in crowded areas such as malls and airports without thinking whom may be listening nearby.

As to telemarketer being able to call cell phones, under the federal Telephone Consumer Protection Act, it is against the law to use auto dialers or prerecorded messages to call numbers assigned to cell phones or pagers.

The only exception is when the person called has previously given their consent. The law does fails to specifically prohibit "live" telemarketing calls to cell phones. Calls from telemarketers can happen, especially if a wire line telephone number is assigned to a cell phone.

With text messaging becoming popular you may be wondering what are the laws in respect to spam and unsolicited bulk advertising. The FCC in 2004 took action to protect wireless subscribers from spam. Under the CAN-SPAM Act, it is prohibit for companies to send commercial messages to

wireless devices, specifically to any addresses that is associated with wireless subscriber messaging services.
Commercial messages can only be sent to individuals who have given their consent.

Wireless networks have made it easier to connect to a network, no matter whether it's the office or home network. But it has also spawned a new past-time among hobbyists and corporate spies called war-driving.

These data voyeurs will drive around a neighborhood or office district using a laptop and free software in an attempt to locate unsecured wireless networks. Signals can be transmitted over a 100 yards from the source. They will capture, with their laptops, the data that is transmitted to and from the network's computers. Within this data could be household finances or business information.

There are many security options available with Wireless network units, but many have some or all of them disabled. This is especially true in the home network.

Not only can data be stolen, altered, or destroyed, but also programs could be put onto computers. More probable extra computers can be added to the unsecured network without your knowledge allowing them free access to the Internet. This risk is highest in densely populated neighborhoods and office building complexes.

With the amount of time that we are using wireless devices it's not hard to forget or maybe not even aware of the dangers involved in wireless devices.

It's important to remember that wireless devices broadcast signals over the air and any receiver that can pick up and understand the signal is able to use the information, not just the device designed to use it.

Technology things to do, but sometimes don't!

There seems to always be things that should be done, but for whatever reason they either slip to the end of the to-do list or simply never gets completed. These are some of those technology things that can and do slide, but shouldn't.

Virus Software:
It is not enough to have it installed on your computer, and if you don't have one the first thing you should do is go out and get it. Virus software must be active to detect virus as they are introduced onto your computer and not as a method of removing the virus once you are infected.

But just as important is to be certain that your virus detector is having it up to date. New viruses are constantly being created. Virus detectors can be set up to do automatic updates. Have your software set up to do it. But be aware of when the updates are scheduled. There must be an active Internet connection. Having it set up to be done at 3 o'clock in the morning when the computer is turned off is just as bad as not having it set up at all.

Backups:
No matter how new or old your computer system may be, it is possible for it to fail. It's bad enough that it may fail and you need to have it repaired, but if that failure occurs in the

hard drive, where your data it stored, you could lose that data.

Backup your data. When? Whenever you have data stored that you cannot afford to lose. The day that you finish an important report needed for advancement in your career could also be the day that your system fails and your data is destroyed.

What do you use to backup? That's not as important as that you do it. You can have another hard drive and have it backed up there. Or you could have the data backed up to a CD or a removable USB drive.

It's also a very good idea to have your data stored in another location than your system. If a fire occurs and destroy your system and the backup is sitting next to it, then it'll be gone too. Multiple backups at multiple locations are a good idea as well.

You may also want to consider backing up your contacts from you cell phone. Cell phones are one of the most often replaced electronic items. Many people store numbers on their phones, because of a call to them, and then forget to put it in any other directory.

Scan computer for hidden Adware and Spyware!
Adware and Spyware are the enemy of a Windows PC. If you don't have some sort of adware or spyware on your computer, it's probably because you aren't on the Internet.

What is Spyware? The term spyware refers to malicious software designed to intercept or take partial control of a

128

computer's operation without the informed consent of that machine's owner. Adware is software that displays advertisements, whether it has the owner consent.

Check your computer. One of the biggest affects of Adware and Spyware on your machines is for it to appear slow. This is because these programs are constantly in use in the background.

Secure data on removal devices!
Removable USB drives makes it easy to move data from one PC to another or to keep backups at another location. But because of their size they are also easy to misplace and lose. If it happens to have all of your private data on it, all of a sudden someone else may be you, having stolen your identity along with your drive.

Some devices now offer data encryption as part of their drives. It's wise to use it.

Has common sense been replaced by rushing?

It's a hectic run here, go there, do that, type of world that many small businesses enjoy. I know we don't enjoy it but it seems to be the way of life.

Because of all our rushing to get work accomplished or be at our child's event, sometimes it seems as if common sense is left behind.

We all seem to be carrying some type of small, or even a big, gadget to assist us in our work. It may be a laptop computer or a digital camera or a MP3 player. Or the no one would leave home or office without one, a cell phone. The one thing we don't want is for that device to be lost or stolen.

Laptop computers, portable storage devices and cell phones will usually have critical and valuable information stored in them. It wouldn't just be a shame if they were lost, but could be damaging to a business.

Many of the following items fall under common sense, but sometimes it does take that gentle reminder to remember them.

To help protect our gadgets from thief.

- Keep them in sight. Don't leave your laptop on the table while you get that second cup of coffee.

- Use bags and carrying cases that don't advertise their contents. Computer bags may be handy, but they let everyone know there's a computer inside.

- Secure devices. Don't leave them clearly visible in a hotel room, use the hotel safe or a security lock/chain wrapped around an unmovable object.

- When leaving them in a vehicle, secure them in the trunk.

- Keep the serial numbers in a safe place. You'll need the number to file a police report and insurance claims.

Life is busy enough doing the things that need to be done. You don't need to add replacing a stolen device to your to-do list.

Other stuff

It's all in the planning!

Do you have a business plan? Most businesses do. But there are other plans that small businesses should have but many times they are not done. There may be many reasons for this. But these plans should be put in place.

A Technology Plan

Technology is ever changing. It's not as bad as it once was when you would purchase the first one off the assembly line and it was already obsolete, but it's still nearly impossible to keep pace with technology.

One of the things to always keep in mind is that you shouldn't purchase technology simply because you believe you want it. Many salespersons will try to sell on that. They will tell you that it will help you. The key is to always know that you need it.

Technology is one of those things that can break a budget in an eye-blink. Having a technology consultant is one way to be able to control the cost. They can evaluate the need.

Since there are so many technology items available that can help you in business, it's important that you prioritize your purchases. Is having the newest smart-phone for you the right thing, if your accounting package is years old and hardly doing the job for you.

The technology plan should be part of your Business Plan. The plan should be a multi-year strategy plan to maintain and upgrade hardware and software. Look at the items that are vital to the successful operation of your business. Keep an eye out for new technology that may be coming and see if it should be incorporated into the plan.

One of the advantages of a plan is that it may help to avoid sticker shock because you'll be able to plan upgrades over a period of time.

Just because you have developed a technology plan doesn't mean that you can't deviate from it. If something is developed that can save money in your course of business, you may just have to delay one of the other items on it.

There are ways that you can save on technology purchases. For items you have in your plan to purchase look for technology sales. Another way is to consider purchasing used.

Unfortunately, many businesses close their doors every day. When a business closes, they may liquidate their capital assets, which could include their technology assets. It's sad to see business fail, but their lost could be your gain.

Technology changes everyday. You want to get your best value from technology investments.

Replacement Plan

Many of us want to have the newest of everything out there. There's nothing wrong with that as long as the technology budget is in place to handle it. Just because something is a few years old doesn't make it worthless.

There are many people who may have purchase a PDA, handheld computer or even a cell phone a few years ago and you couldn't get them to give it up for anything.

As long as it's getting the job done, and not causing you more problems than it's worth, having older technology may be best. While it's a good idea to have a replacement plan it doesn't mean a gadget in perfect working order needs to be discarded.

With any gadget one thing will nearly always happen. It will stop working. It may stop because the battery that came with it goes dead, or will refuse to recharge. Or it may because you forgot to take your cell phone off of your person in the restroom and it found some standing water.

The question is, do I have it fixed or do I replace it?

You can ask, How dead is it? A bad battery can be replaced. But one that took a swim in the toilet the decision is easy. That one gets replaced

The next question is how much does it cost? That would be the cost for the repair as well as the cost for replacement. A replacement cell phone battery may cost $ 30.00, but you maybe able to get a new cell phone for just a few dollars more.

There could be an added cost to that. You will probably have to renew your contract. That's no big deal if you are satisfied with your service and planning to continue after your current contract. However if you are unhappy with service and thinking about leaving for another carrier, you may not want to go that route.

Some people use a simple rule to determine the time to replace or repair. If it costs less than 50% of the cost of new, do the repair otherwise purchase new.

This does seem to be a good rule of thumb and most times you may be better off doing it that way. That is unless the piece is more than a few years old. Then I look at the cost to repair should be less than 50%-10% for each additional year. A three-year-old item is time to replace if it's more than 20% of the cost of a new one to repair. By the time it's three years old it's probably three version or more behind anyway.

Sometimes you can get lucky. If you are good with your hands and have some knowledge of technology you may be able to fix it yourself. If that's the case the cost for repair could be way down since you only have to pay for the parts. Your time is free. But is it? I guess you may need to figure how valuable is your time and whether it's worth your while to repair.

The best plan though is to always have a replacement plan, that in itself may give you the answer.

A Disaster recovery Plan

It doesn't matter the size of a business, if a disaster happens it's going to hurt. Having a plan may help alleviate the pain.

The IT and Telecom (or as I like to refer to them Telephony) infrastructures are a couple of the major items to consider in disaster recovery. If you lose your Internet connection or your telephones how critical is this to getting your job done. A sales based organization these could be critical parts of the organization. A plan is needed.

One of the best ways to prevent downtime of these services is to have redundancy. If everything is on one circuit coming into your building then it's just like the old adage having all your eggs in the same basket. If you drop the basket all of the eggs may break. If your Voice and Internet is all on the same circuit, if that's lost there's no communications.

By having redundancy, even if you aren't at full operation, you aren't at No operation. Redundancy can and usually does have an added cost, but that added cost is similar to paying insurance.

It may seem like a waste when paying it, but when you need it, it's a welcome relief.

A recovery plan needs to cover all items of the network, data or voice. This includes the instrument on the desk, the common equipment such as data server or telephone system, to the connection to the public.

Spring Ahead to Fall back - DST

In the spring, as it does every year just like Christmas and Tax day, Daylight Saving Time begins. For those who don't know the rhyme we spring ahead an hour in the spring and fall backward one hour, in the fall. Some people mistakenly call it Daylight Savings time, but it is Daylight Saving Time.

In 1986 the dates for DST in the US was established as the first Sunday in April and the Last Sunday in October. In 2007 with the Energy Policy Act of 2005 that President George Bush signed into law in 2005, the new dates for Daylight Saving Time will begin on the second Sunday of March and end the first Sunday of November.

It all depends on who is asked whether Daylight Saving Time is a good idea or not. One study done in the 1970s by the U.S Department of transportation shows that the country's electricity usage is cut by about one percent each day with Daylight Saving Time.

Why is this? One of the biggest uses of energy is for electricity for lighting our homes. By moving the clocks ahead in the spring, it gets darker later in the day and the need for lights in the house are less, since they need to come on later. Also with sunlight later in the day, the plans for outdoor activities rise meaning less electricity would be used, since people aren't in the house to use it.

Daylight Saving Start and end dates beginning in 2007.

Year	Begins 2nd Sunday in March	Ends 1st Sunday in November
2007	March 11	November 4
2008	March 9	November 2
2009	March 8	November 1
2010	March 14	November 7
2011	March 13	November 6
2012	March 11	November 4
2013	March 10	November 3
2014	March 9	November 2
2015	March 8	November 1

Unlike it was years ago, when I use to have a list of clocks that I needed to manually set when I arrived early to work on the Monday after DST change, many systems will automatically reset to the correct time. With the change of the dates for DST, it is possible older devices will not change correctly. Hopefully by March of 2007, patches for systems will be developed otherwise you may be setting clocks again.

Daylight Saving Time is not a modern idea. Benjamin Franklin first mentioned it in a letter to the Journal of Paris in 1784. It wasn't put into practice until the German government put it in place in 1916.

The U.S. Congress established it at the same time they formally adopted the Rail Road Time Zones in 1918. It became so unpopular that the law for DST time was repealed in 1919.

In 1942, during World War II, DST was reinstated in the U.S. although from the end of the war in 1945 until 1966, there wasn't a Federal that addressed DST.

In 1966 DST was established and has been in place since, although the law gave states the capability to exempt themselves and a few, such as Arizona and Hawaii have. Many countries follow some sort of DST plan.

Hopefully your clock will be changed correctly. If not you'll be walking into work an hour late on Monday in the spring or an hour early in the fall.

Along with the change of clocks with DST, Fire departments recommend that the battery in fire and smoke detectors be changed. There are studies that show that a working smoke detector can more than double a person's chances of surviving a home fire.

It's estimated that as many as 1/3 of the homes with smoke detectors have dead or missing batteries.

5 things to do after getting a new computer.

1) Create an Administrators and a Users account. Use the user account for normal work and use the Administrators account only when required.

2) Turn on the operating system's firewall. This firewall is strong enough to help prevent many problems.

3) Install and activate Anti-Virus software. Set it up to receive automatic updates at a time you know the computer will be connected to the Internet

Each of the above items **SHOULD** be done before connecting to the Internet

4) Update software. This would include your Operating System as well as your Anti-Virus.

5) Be proactive against spyware. It's better to have the protection before you get infected than trying to remove it once it is installed.

10 Hi-Tech items to consider

Small businesses need to take advantage of advances in technology. Technology can be used to increase productivity and reduce costs. It may be remote working or just the availably of instant communications.

Just be prepared some of these may also place you in greater dependence of providers of hi-tech products and services to help them keep connected. Use these to help you stay connected:

1) Broadband – Everyday more resources are becoming available on the World Wide Web. A Broadband connection keeps you from waiting on slow page downloads. It is important for the office, but depending on your business, having it at home may be just as valuable.

2) Internet banking – Nearly all banks now offer a way to do your banking on the Internet. Transfer money between accounts or check balances. These are all less time consuming then going to your neighborhood bank. You can use it to make payments and accept on-line payments as while.

3) Internet PR – With the advent of the concept of key-words used by search engines, the possible need for an

Internet PR firm may be helpful to have those looking for services that you provide to be sent to your website and not another's.

4) Internet telephony or VoIP – The nature of communicating by voice is changing. Many VoIP providers are offering long distance calls for nearly no charge. It's just a matter of converting the analog audio signals to digital data and using the Internet connection. However you do need to keep an eye on the services, what today may be free may cost tomorrow. Charges are forever changing in the tele-communication environment. When requirements change so do the charges

5) Online networking – The Internet has made it easy to network with like-minded business people. There may be nothing better than the face-to-face meeting, but the Internet can be used to quickly obtain potential leads and other information. It's a good place to help build solid business relationships.

6) On-demand software - Small business owners work from many locations. Software once was delivered on a desk or CD. Now updates can be downloaded from the Internet. Even the software itself can be. Some can even be downloaded and used free of charge. You can store data in on-line secured storage for access no matter where you may be.

7) Podcasting – Do you spend a significant amount of time commuting, running, or in the gym? It could be time to make use of that time by listening to podcasts.

The term podcast refers to both the content (i.e. multimedia files such as MP3 music files) and delivery mechanism (via Internet to mobile device such as iPod or PC). You can use Podcasts as a great way to learn or a way of communicating with your prospects and customers.

8) Really Simple Syndication (RSS) - Thousands of pages of valuable news, views, tips and tricks are published everyday. Instead of having to remember your favorite website for information, you can have them deliver the information to you. That's what RSS feeds achieve. All you need is a newsreader.

9) Smartphones - This is an electronic handheld device that integrates mobile phone, personal organizer and Internet access tools into one. While often more expensive than traditional cell phones, they do offer flexibility. These could save you a lot of time by allowing you to be available while not in the office.

10) Wi-Fi connects you on the move – Many of the same reason you need Broadband you may also need Wi-Fi. If your office is equipped with a Wi-Fi connection, it's just a matter of firing up your laptop and you can begin work. Or you may have a vendor coming from miles away and he has a Wi-Fi connected laptop. He can get online and receive the information you may need immediately instead of waiting. Also for small fee, even at times for free, you may be able to do work from major coffee shops and other meeting places.

What is RFID?

Radio Frequency Identification (RFID) is an identification method, relying on storing and retrieving data using devices called tags. An RFID tag is a small object that is attached or incorporated into a product, animal, or person. RFID tags contain silicon chips that enable them to receive and respond to queries from an RFID transceiver.

An RFID system consists of several components including tags, tag readers, and application software.

The data transmitted by the tag may provide identification or location information, or specifics about the product tagged, such as price, color, date of purchase, etc.

The use of RFID in tracking and access applications first appeared during the 1980s. RFID quickly gained attention because of its ability to track moving objects

RFID tags can be passive, semi-passive (also known as semi-active), or active.

Passive
Passive RFID tags have no internal power supply. Passive tags have practical read distances up to a few feet. Passive RFID tags do not require batteries, and can be much smaller

and have an unlimited life span. Because passive tags are cheaper to manufacture and have no battery, the majority of RFID tags in existence are of the passive variety.

Semi-passive

Semi-passive RFID tags are very similar to passive tags except for the addition of a small battery. This battery allows the tag IC to be constantly powered. Semi-passive RFID tags are faster in response.

Active

Unlike passive and semi-passive RFID tags, active RFID tags have their own internal power supply and are typically beacon tags, but can also be used as response tags. Beacon tags are so named because they transmit their tag data and ID at a predetermined fixed interval. Whereas, "response" tags only respond when an active RFID reader requests the tags to transmit.

These tags are being used in many places to keep track of inventory. Wal-Mart is one of the biggest users of RFID's.

Saving Energy and using Technology

Energy costs are rising. It doesn't matter whether it's the price of gas, or the cost of electric.

We all know that using technology also uses energy. If it doesn't run directly off of electricity it runs off of a battery that needs to be charged.

Here are some things you can do to help save energy. Some of these are saving while using technology; others are using technology to save.

1) Charge battery operated devices such as a cell phone while in your automobile. If you spend a lot of time in your car, you can use it to charge batteries. A cell phone many times will charge in less time using a vehicle charger than one used in the office powered by electric.

2) Use Audio or Video conferencing instead of traveling.

3) Turn off or set office equipment to power down when not in use. Turning off one computer and monitor nightly and on weekends could save up to $80 a year. It's a good idea to set PCs, monitors and copiers to use sleep mode when not in use.

4) Choose ENERGY STAR® products when upgrading or adding new equipment. These products meet federal standard for energy efficiency, and are often available at the same cost as less efficient models.

5) Reduce lighting where possible and take advantage of natural daylight. Turning lights off or dimming them during the day allows for lower energy costs.

6) Install occupancy sensors, timers, or photocells to ensure that interior and exterior lights are turned off at the appropriate time. These devices can reduce lighting costs by turning off lights in unoccupied areas.

7) Replace incandescent bulbs with compact fluorescent lamps (CFLs), which can last up to ten times longer. CFLs provide the same amount of light as standard incandescent bulbs, but uses less energy.

8) By having equipment turned off or in low energy modes during periods of inactivity those items are generating less heat. Fluorescent bulbs and lamps as well as LED generate less heat than incandescent lights. This saves on air conditioning costs.

9) Install programmable thermostats or time clocks to automatically control temperature settings on heating and air conditioning equipment. Adjust the thermostat down in the winter and up in the summer and shut off when not in use. Even a few degrees can significantly reduce heating and air conditioning costs.

Using Batteries Safely

One thing we all need to be aware, while batteries are a way of today's life, they need to be used and disposed of properly. Batteries are made of chemicals and many of these chemicals can be dangerous to us and can cause a hazard to the environment.

Once the useful life of any battery ends, be certain to dispose of it in the proper manner. The elements that are used in batteries Nickel Cadmium (Ni-Cd), Nickel Metal Hydride (Ni-MH), Lithium Ion (Li-ion) and Small Sealed Lead (Pb) in items such as cordless power tools, cellular and cordless phones, laptop computers, camcorders, digital cameras, and remote control toys should be recycled and not thrown in the trash.

Here's some safety tips for use of batteries.

1) Never dispose of batteries in a fire. They may rupture, releasing internal ingredients. Batteries need to be disposed of properly.

2) Promptly remove dead or weak batteries from devices. These batteries could leak dangerous chemicals.

3) Never mix old and new batteries in a device. Battery leakage may occur. Replace all of the batteries in a device at the same time.

4) Never mix battery types in a device. Examples of battery types are alkaline, heavy duty, rechargeable.

5) Recharge batteries in the charger designed for the battery.

6) Carefully install batteries in the correct polarity direction (+ and -) as instructed by the manufacturer.

7) Do not leave battery powered devices switched "on" after the batteries are exhausted. Battery leakage may occur.

8) If a device is to be stored for a long period the batteries should be removed.

9) Store batteries in a cool, dry location. Avoid temperature extremes. Keep batteries in original package until you are ready to use them.

Many modern laptop computers use a battery chemistry of Lithium-Ion. Lithium batteries actually started back in 1912 but didn't become commercially available until after 1970. Rechargeable Lithium batteries were made in the 1980's, but failed due to safety reasons.

Research since has uncovered inherent dangers in the design of a lithium metal electrode battery and focus has shifted to using non-metal electrodes and lithium ions. These batteries have less energy density than the full metal electrode variety, but are inherently a lot safer, and have found their way to being one of the most popular battery chemistries currently.

But Lithium-Ion batteries are sensitive to discharge and charge conditions, and will have protection built into the battery. They do not tolerate overcharge and charging must be stopped once it reaches full charge.

Lithium-Ion batteries do not suffer from the same memory effect as NiCd batteries and they have a much higher energy density.

Additionally Lithium-Ion batteries have a useful life of 3 years from day of manufacture. Battery temperature above 40C or 104F can lead to reduced capacity. They will lose about 10% of their charge per month.

It's possible to use Lithium-Ion batteries without any dangers, but they need to be used property. The electronics involved should prevent accidents from happening, but users need to not allow the batteries to discharge below about 30% capacity on a daily basis, otherwise battery capacity can be affected.

This is one battery that shallow discharges is actually better for the life of the battery.

Working with and learning to use a "gadget"

A cell phone, a digital camera, a MP3 player, all of these are gadgets of choice for one who wants to stay up-to-date in the use of technology.

Whether you have one device that has them all, or one of each, the common element is that you need to learn to use it. Otherwise it's just a useless gadget, and with the cost some of them have, also a waste of money.

For some, learning to use an electronic device is second nature, something that comes naturally. To others it's repeatedly being shown how to use it and still not being able to use it correctly. How many blinking clocks have you seen on VCR's over the years?

There may be many reasons for how well someone readily accepts something new. Many of us are use to putting a round disc shaped object; a CD or a vinyl record, into a player and out comes music.

Even a tape has moving objects. Now to hear music, we take a computer file, play it on the computer or move it to a small device and listen with headphones.

We are used to holding a roll of film that holds 24-36 pictures. No wonder some of us have problems with a couple of hundred pictures being stored on a piece of postage stamp size plastic.

Things could come clearer to us if we didn't already have preconceived notions. Perhaps that is why the young has a lot less trouble accepting things that are new. They don't have preconceived ideas.

Studies have found that the youth of today, which may have always been the case, do not feel as if they are a value. But if you want to find out what will be important in our future, ask them. They aren't afraid of technology and want it.

It may be time for us to tap into that resource? We may be having problems figuring out how to work our cell phone or digital camera, but a lot of times they have it mastered before the first battery is discharged. Let's ask them for help. It will help with their self-esteem and we may just learn something.

IM for Business?

There are plenty of ways to instantly get in touch with someone. You can use the telephone to call. You can send an email. But are you using Instant Messaging as part of your normal business practice?

Instant Messaging or IM has for years been popular with the younger generation. At first it was using the computer and then through Texting on cell phones. But have you been using it? I have to admit I haven't, even though I believe that I should be.

Some may think that IM is one of those gadgets that actually take away from our busy schedule. They have this opinion because the use of IM is opening us up for disruption from anyone that knows our screen name.

Friends and family will be contacting us for anything at anytime. Do you really want to be disturbed by Cousin Ernie asking if you are ready for the weekend fishing trip?

But is that really any different than the telephone? Who wouldn't want a telephone in the office? Friends and family have the same opportunity to contact you. They don't because they understand that to contact when working it should be an emergency. And to a newlywed wife to call her husband to say I love and miss you to her is an emergency.

IM can be the same. After hours you can talk and chat with whomever about whatever you want, but let your friends and family know that during business hours it has to be an emergency. If they want to know what's an emergency, just say if the message is not important enough to call on the telephone then it's not important enough to IM.

You can select the hours you want for business IM's. Some of us may only want the business time as 9 to 5; others may want it from 7 to 7. Only you know your business schedule.

Where do you find IM software? It's probably already on your computer. Microsoft, Yahoo and AOL each have their own version. There are others as well. At present they aren't interchangeable with one another, but in the future that may change.

AOL seems to have a bigger following in the younger generation and Yahoo to the older. It may not be true, but it is the way that I perceive it. I've use all three of those at times, but none of them for business and a couple of these not in awhile.

It's not hard to use. All you need to do is create a screen name, log into their system and wait for someone to send you a message. You can create two screen names if you wish, one for business and one for after hours.

If you protect your IM screen name the same as you do your telephone number, why would you expect it to be any more disturbing than the telephone.

Using IM in Business?

Instant Messaging is not new. In the early days of the Internet revolution it was used as a way for people all over the world to talk to one another with out having to use the telephone and the costs associated with those calls. It was free and easy.

But because of the perceived ills of IM, it has not been readily accepted in many businesses. Some of this was because managers would see lost production when employees were Internet chatting as they worked, or instead of working. Some have even banned these services from even residing on the computer.

But if used correctly and under control of the managers with good policies and procedures, IM can be a productive tool.

Some uses of IM:

Ask a quick question – Many times an email may be written, or a phone call placed to an associate in another office to ask a question. By sending the person an IM many times that question is answered faster and since they have answered in text, the answer is precise and understood.

Collaboration – When working on a project remotely, doing IM collaboration is quicker than email and easier than by telephone. The text is there and can be copied into the document.

Improve customer service – When used property the customer can feel assured of answers to their question. They can read again the answer and if they have additional questions, they can be raised. With voice communications, they may need you to repeat the answer a couple of times. The customer can also save the text and review it at a later time.

There are some risks when using IM. As with any Internet related technology it is subjected to attacks, such as viruses, worms and phishing scams. But when used with a well develop policy, IM can be an effective business tool.

Create an IM Policy

It doesn't matter whether you use Instant Messaging in your business or not, there should be a policy regarding its use. Without a policy, the employees won't know the company's feeling about it, and they will often make their own decisions on if and how it's used. Having a policy in place will not only protect them, but the company as well.

When creating an IM policy use these items to get it started.

1) Decide whether or not the company will allow IMs.

2) Standardize on one service. Everyone has their preferred service, but the company needs to be the one to determine which is best for them.

3) Determine what type of information should and should not be transmitted via IM sessions.

4) Define limits on the use of IM. Include in the policy how personal IMs are to be handled.

5) Control the user name. The user name should be appropriate for business use. Since it will be used for business communication, the company and not the user should have authority over the user name.

6) Save IM messages.

7) Detail the risks that are involved in using IM software.

8) Define content in the policy. A policy should be in place detailing what's allowed in any written communication, even letters and email. Items to address include the use of profanity, sexual references and confidential business or personal information.

9) Review the IM policy and practice on a regular schedule. Internet security changes quickly and changes may be required in the policy.

10) Detail punishment for not adhering to the policy. With any policy, all members of the company should follow it and be punished for violations equally. Have the employee read, understand and sign the policy to prevent misunderstandings.

How's your consumer service?

AOL has gotten a bad press due to a recording of a consumer trying to cancel their service.

Comcast fired a service tech for taking a nap on a consumer's couch while waiting for over an hour for assistance. He was waiting for assistance from his own company. Granted he shouldn't have been sleeping, but don't you think that the company wouldn't have wanted him to waiting for help that long. He was on the payroll.

No matter your product, shouldn't consumer service be a part of it.

How is your consumer service and the technology you use?

Is your telephone answered? On the 2nd ring, 4th or does the answering machine (voice mail) answer?

Do you return emails, even it's just to say, 'I need a little more time to get you the answer'?

Is your web page up-to-date? Does it have the correct contact information and services available?

You have reached ...

Every one of us will at one time, or many times a day be greeted by a voice mail message. Some of us may get frustrated with either the fact we reached a person's voice mail, or expecting the familiar voice of the one you are calling and not having them answer.

Believe it or not Voice Mail when used effectively, can improve communications, eliminate telephone tag, and improve customer service.

When making a telephone call it's advisable keep the following in mind.

1) Be prepared to leave a detailed message. It's nice to have the bit of chit-chat with some one you are calling but be aware you may get voice mail and plan what you want to say before you call.

2) Speak clearly and slowly. Some people seem to speak faster when leaving messages on voice mail, and those are harder to understand.

3) Leave a concise message spelling out reason for calling. If applicable leave referral names and mention mutual business associates. Don't deliver bad news via voicemail.

4) Always ask for a call back. Give a day and time you'd be available to receive their call back

5) Mention your name and phone number at the beginning and end of each message.

It's also important to keep these in mind when you are recording a greeting message.

1) Your caller was expecting you to answer, let them know that they have reached a recording.

2) Let your caller know your availability. If you are out of the office for a few days tell them so they won't be expecting a call later that day.

3) If you have a time limit on the length that some one can leave a message let them know. Don't tell them to leave a detailed message, if there's a possibly that they may be disconnect.

4) If applicable give the caller a chance to be connected with someone else. Be certain that person will be available. It's bad enough to tell your caller you are on vacation, but worst if the person you refer them to, is also on vacation.

5) Always return your calls.

Voice Mail is a valuable tool. Used correctly it's a benefit to business, but used incorrectly it can be a disaster.

How's your email etiquette?

Email is becoming a common way of to communicate, but some people forget there is the right and wrong way to use it.

1. Be polite. Some people will send an email with a demanding tone. Emails to friends are all right to be silly, but professional emails should always be professional. Address them as seems proper, if in doubt don't use first names, but titles. If responding back to someone who signed off with their first name, it's probably ok for you to address them as such. Don't make an email longer than it needs to be.

2. Check for spelling and grammar mistakes. Don't type an email message and send it off without reviewing its contents, you may have just told your stockbroker to sell when you meant to say do not sell. Don't use 'short-hand' codes. While it may be to an advantage to use U instead of 'you' or R instead of 'are' in a text message, it should never be used in an email.

3. Don't leave out details, but at the same time don't put in to much information. When asking a question or requesting information, give enough details so that your recipient will understand your request,

but not too much information that they won't bother to read it. When replying to an email that was sent to you, answer all of the questions in the email. Some times the first question is answered, but one later in the email wasn't, possibly because it wasn't read. It's also a good idea to send information for questions not asked, but you suspect may follow.

4.   Use the proper type of email address for the type of email being sent. It may be all right to send your friend an email from 2sexy4u, but would you want to send an email using that to a prospective employer or an employee.

5.   Watch the use of attachments. Attachments have become the bane of many email users. Over the years attachments may have contained viruses and the common practice is not to open attachments unless you have requested someone to send a file or know they may be sending one. Some companies may even filter out some or all attachments before they reach the recipient. You may even be violating copyright laws by forwarding certain attachments sent to you.

6.   Use the subject line intelligently. Tell the person to whom you are sending the email, the reason for the email in the subject line. People get many emails in a day. Many of them are unwanted. While Hi may be a nice greeting it means nothing to someone just looking at the subject lines in emails to see which

ones to respond. It also is a common filter for junk emails.

7. Use email responsibly. Do not use CAPITAL LET-TERS. To many this is interpreted as shouting. Use the proper layout and short paragraphs with blank lines between each paragraphs makes an email easier to read. Email programs have an option of sending an email as high priority. Many people ignore priority in email messages, and some may even see a high-priority message as slightly aggressive and act. It's best not to send it this way unless you know the one you are sending it to wants you to use it. Watch what you forward. Some people may be comfortable sending you information, but may not want others to know. Refrain from requesting delivery and read receipts, they may be annoying to the recipient. Don't attempt to recall a message, it has probably already been delivered. It's better to send a second email acknowledging your mistake.

8. Answer your emails within a reasonable amount of time, but don't continue the email chain by returning one when a response is no longer required.

9. It's a good idea to keep the message thread. The message thread is the prior emails of the same subject. Some people think that since an earlier email was sent, the prior information is not needed. People receive many emails each day, and may not remember all of the details of prior messages. By keeping the thread intact, they can quickly review the topic.

10. Address emails correctly. If sending out an informational email to many different people, use the Bcc: field. It's not always advisable to use the Bcc: field instead of the Cc: field. Blind copy only when it's necessary. Some people don't like their email address passed around without their permission. If addressing too many people in the To: field, that is what's happening. Watch the usage of Cc: field. Many people may not realize they were simply copied on the email and not act upon the message. Beware using the Reply to: or the Reply to All:. Only reply to those who need to see your reply. This goes double if you are you are replying to an email sent by a subordinate to criticize their email.

Make a good impression. In some cases an email may be the first and only correspondence you may have with someone. If you spend time in putting together a well-written message, it will show.

And remember once you hit the send button, it's too late to make changes.

An email policy can give the dos and don'ts about how your company uses email. It will give employees a full understanding of the importance of proper email usage.

May I help you? Thank you!

Sometimes we are more concerned about using technology and using it correctly we forget that it's really only a tool.

Ask yourself these questions and see if you answer Yes to any of them.

Have you called someone and heard them typing in the background? Did they seem more interested in doing other tasks, than talking with you?

Have you registered at a hotel or rented a car and the clerk ended the conversation with 'you're all set now', but never heard a 'Thank You'?

Have you been talking to someone who reached for his or her cell phone and answered it, while still in mid-conversation with you?

Have you been distributed during a movie or a quiet dinner by a ringing cell phone? By one with an annoying ring?

Have you thought someone was speaking to you only to find they were talking on their cell phone?

Now, the most important question of all. Have you been guilty of one or more of these? If you were honest with yourself the answer would be yes to some, maybe even all of the questions.

It seems that old-fashioned courtesy is a thing of the past. But should it be?

Don't you feel better when you call a service provider and they ask 'How can I help you?' and end the call with 'Thank You".

Isn't it time that you do the same?

Afterword
Or
Who's Who in Telecom

Once upon a time whenever one wanted to communicate with someone on the other end of the country, a telephone was picked up, a number dialed, just one number to reach an operator. There was a nice friendly voice on the other end of the line, whose native language was the same as yours. You asked to be connected to a party and a few minutes later you had that person on the line. Everyone was happy.

But not everyone was happy, and it was decided that this communications bliss wasn't good for business. I'm not sure whose business, but a federal judge made it his business and decided there was a monopoly. The company, the biggest telecommunications company in the world, one that was innovated and always at work to make things better for the user, was required to divide its company.

There may have been others smaller parts that were broken away, but those that all could see was the formation of seven regional telephone company. Their purpose was to supply telephone service to the users in their region. The parent could supply services to communicate over great distances.

There were a couple of smaller companies who had been trying to supply long distance, but it was envisioned now they would be on a more even playing field.

People were still bind by wires and more and more wanted to communicate wirelessly, which up had been used mostly by police, fire, other governmental agencies and taxis. The FCC, the all-seeing body of the airways, established in the 1930's by a telecommunications act of congress, the act still exists today, made a plan.

There was money out there to be gained by selling off the radio frequency spectrum. This new natural resource of the US, which had been around freely in the air since time began, could be had by a price. A plan was made that would use a cellular approach to radio waves.

Is wireless communications a good thing? That can be debated and could make an entire another discussion. But the point to be said here is that these were created to be separate.

Time passed and the seven regional companies combined to make four. And each had a piece of the wireless pie. But they wanted more. They wanted long distance. So they followed the rules that the congress and FCC set up and became long distance carriers themselves.

But was that enough, apparently not since mergers have been escalating to an unbelievable degree in the past couple of years. ATT wireless, which only held the ATT name and not part of the corporation, merged with Cingular, who at one time was known as CellOne. A name I think is better than Cingular.

Sprint and Nextel merged, creating another big wireless player, instead of two smaller ones.

Then what was unthinkable in 1984 the baby bell had finally gotten to be bigger than the bad old mother and SBC merged with ATT. They took the name and AT&T was reborn.

Verizon not wanting to be left behind merged with MCI, after a long battle with Qwest on who would get the once 2nd biggest long distance carrier. And it's probably not over.

Are the current treads of telecom mergers good for the future of telecommunication? From a business stance it may be, but we should also remember what happen to WorldCom.

But the worst part about all of these telecom mergers is that soon the Daytona 500 will just be a Sprint race.

About The Author

Steven G. (Steve) Atkinson has over twenty-five years of telecommunications experience. He has worked as a RF and Technical Specialist and has worked with various governmental agencies with their needs relating to telecommunication.

He worked as the Telecommunication Manager at a small college, managing the telephone system used by the Faculty, Staff and Students. There he learned the value of listening to the students on how they use and what is expected of technology. They will be the business owners and leaders of tomorrow.

He is the owner and chief consultant at E-S Technology Consulting, based on Maryland's Eastern Shore, currently assisting small businesses with technology.

He regularly publishes Technology Tips for Small Business at his site, tt4sb.com. Those posts were the initial source of many of these tips.

Mr. Atkinson can be contacted at sgatkinson@tt4sb.com.

www.ingramcontent.com/pod-product-compliance
Lightning Source LLC
Chambersburg PA
CBHW031935190326
41519CB00007B/543